Links to Learning

A Curriculum Planning Guide for After-School Programs

National Institute on Out-of-School Time
Wellesley Centers for Women

A Publication of School-Age NOTES

National Institute on Out-of-School Time
Wellesley Centers for Women
Wellesley College
106 Central Street
Wellesley, MA 02481
(781) 283-2547 / www.niost.org

Cover and book design by: **Diane Neel, DNGraphics**, Nashville, TN
Photos by: **Craig Burleigh**, Belmont, CA
Published by: **School-Age NOTES**
                          P.O. Box 40205
                          Nashville, TN 37204
                          1-800-410-8780

Table of Contents

Table of Contents

Table of Contents

Table of Contents

This book is dedicated to Rich Scofield,
whose passion, hope, and energy
inspired a whole generation of us
to stand up for young people.

Acknowledgements

The National Institute on Out-of-School Time (NIOST) gratefully acknowledges the collaborative efforts of so many individuals in the creation of this *Links to Learning Curriculum Planning Guide*.

First and foremost to Barbara Taylor, Senior Consultant for Program Development at the YMCA of the USA, and Michael Fournier of the Providence YMCA for recognizing and inspiring the need for an earlier version of this Guide: *The YMCA Curriculum Framework*. We appreciate their support and willingness to share their work with the after-school field at large.

With gratitude to Susan O'Connor for her contributions regarding the Links to Learning approach and her valuable strategies for embedding academics into enrichment activities and to Tony Streit and Wendy Rivenburgh of the Education Development Center, Inc. whose contributions to the technology section greatly enhanced this Guide.

We especially want to acknowledge the team efforts of the NIOST staff in consistently going beyond the call of duty, dedicating countless hours of planning and research. To Ellen Gannett, we thank her for her inspiring and encouraging editorial input; to Joyce Shortt, Kathy Schleyer, Eileen Erskine, Genevieve Solomon, Teri Hsueh, Samantha Harris, Jean Wellington and Tasj-Nicole Yabut who helped keep us on track throughout the development of this project with their editorial and administrative support.

We extend a special recognition to Kim Bohen for organizing our thoughts and early drafts into a final product. Kim dedicated countless hours to the writing and editing of this Guide. We are so grateful for her outstanding contribution to making our Guide truly "user-friendly!"

Finally, we thank our own David Alexander, the primary author of this Guide, who has spent the greater part of the past four years immersed in this and the YMCA version of the Guide. We celebrate his capable leadership and creativity. His zest for working with young people and the after-school staff who lead them every day shines brightly throughout this Guide.

We hope that this book will also shine a light on all of you, our readers, who are committed to improving the quality of after-school programs for all our children and youth.

Introduction

School, after-school programs, home, peers and community – each of these worlds shape the lives of young people. Ideally, the time children and youth spend at out-of-school programs can be both complementary and compensatory to the other aspects of their lives. In the current climate of high stakes testing, after-school programs are coming under increased pressure to become academic in nature – more of an extended school day. This is true in spite of growing knowledge about the multiple dimensions of child development, the different ways children learn, and the diverse set of skills they need to be successful in the world.

"Links to Learning" is a training developed by the National Institute on Out-of-School Time (NIOST) to assist out-of-school time providers in responding to the call for after-school academics, while addressing the full range of children's developmental needs. Building on the latest research on resiliency, engagement and motivation, this training is designed to help after-school providers understand how their program activities can intentionally connect the multiple worlds of children and youth and optimally support their development and learning.

This *Curriculum Planning Guide* can be coupled with the NIOST "Links to Learning" training or used by itself. The Guide provides an overview of learning and child development as they relate to out-of-school time programs; offers tips and tools for selecting, planning, developing and evaluating after-school activities; and demonstrates how to link these activities to sample learning and quality standards. It also introduces the reader to curriculum resources focusing on seven "key learning areas" believed to be central to comprehensive, high-quality, after-school programs:

- **Literacy**
- **Science**
- **Math Problem Solving**
- **Arts**
- **Social Competence**
- **Fitness and Nutrition**
- **Technology**

Each "key learning area" section includes one detailed activity plan explicitly linked to learning benchmarks and quality standards. Each section also includes other sample activities and additional resources.

By understanding how children learn and what they need to learn, and by designing activities that meet their developmental needs – as well as quality and learning standards – after-school programs can support the optimal growth and development of children and youth in their care.

Out-of-school time is bursting with opportunities for learning. Informed by an understanding of how children learn and what is important for their development, after-school programs can design myriad opportunities for children and youth to extend and enhance their learning and development beyond the school day. This Links to Learning Guide provides after-school program staff with guidance and tools to create learning opportunities that are different from school but contribute in vital ways to the optimal cognitive, social, emotional and physical development of children and youth – ultimately contributing to their success in school and beyond.

Use this Curriculum Planning Guide to:

- Develop an understanding of learning styles and child development that can impact the selection, planning, implementation and evaluation of after-school activities.

- Find tools that help link chosen after-school activities to learning benchmarks and quality standards.

- Review sample project-based learning activities in seven key learning areas: literacy, science, math, problem solving, arts, social-competence, fitness and nutrition and technology.

- Learn how to develop and access additional sources of high quality, child-centered, inquiry-based after-school curriculum and activities.

Discussion Questions for Section One

1. Share your own childhood experiences associated with after-school time. What did you do after school when you were young? Think about different ages and stages of your development. What were the qualities each experience had? What did you like doing the most? The least?

2. How would you characterize the learning that you did during these times? Does any of it relate to the seven core content areas addressed in this guide, e.g. literacy, science, math, arts, social competence, fitness and nutrition or technology?

Section Two: . . . .
Theoretical Framework - Learning and Development

What Do We Want Children and Youth to Learn?

Using What We Know about Learning
- Learning Styles
- Factors that Influence Attention for Learning
- Guidelines for Transforming to a Child-Centered Approach

Using What We Know About Child Development
- Age and Development
- Resiliency and Developmental Assets

NOTES

Links to Learning: *A Curriculum Planning Guide for After-School Programs*

Section Two
Theoretical Framework - Learning and Development

Though recent research in psychology, education and medicine has taught us a great deal about how children learn and grow, some age-old, common sense understanding remains. Most importantly, we have known for a long time that children need to develop not only cognitively, but also physically, emotionally and socially to succeed in life. Out-of-school (OST) time programs are uniquely suited to bolster children's growth in these other critical developmental areas. Research has also borne out knowledge we have from experience that children, like adults, learn in many different ways. Schools tend to emphasize visual and/or analytical learning. Children who learn best through other means - physical, experiential, interpersonal, artistic, auditory - have a harder time succeeding in traditional classrooms and may become turned off to school, thereby limiting their life choices. If OST programs too closely resemble schools, they may miss out on important opportunities to help children and youth discover their unique talents, passions and abilities. While after-school programs should not look or feel like school, they should be rich in learning opportunities that can attract and sustain participation from all children, including those who may not excel in school.[1]

What Do We Want Children and Youth to Learn?

In addition to the developmental reasons to question the wisdom of making after-school programs more academic, there is also a growing consensus that the kinds of skills necessary to succeed in the 21st century are not confined to "reading, writing and arithmetic." In their book, *Teaching the New Basic Skills*, researchers Frank Levy and Richard Murname came up with a list of skills that there is wide consensus that young people need to succeed in the modern economy, many of which the authors argue traditional schools are not providing: [2]

- Literacy: effectively writing, reading text and data, listening, locating and creating information.

- Numeracy: understanding how numbers represent objects and amounts.

- Written and oral communication: sharing thoughts or ideas with others in many forms.

- Problem solving and critical thinking: not just mathematical problems but everyday questions.

---

[1] See: Sam Piha and Beth Miller, "Getting the Most from After-School: The Role of After-School Programs in a High Stakes Learning Environment," Cross-Cities Network for Leaders of Citywide After-School Initiatives, July 2003. http://www.niost.org/CCN.pdf

[2] Levy, Frank and Richard J. Murname, *Teaching the New Basic Skills*, Free Press. 1996.

- Knowledge of and comfort with technology: use of computers, electronic messages, machines and devices.

- Ability to work with diverse groups of people: comfort, skill and a desire to get along with and work collaboratively or cooperatively with people representing different ethnic, intellectual, philosophical, spiritual and experiential backgrounds.

One of the unfortunate by-products of the high stakes testing environment in public education is that schools lose the flexibility to focus on many of the broader social and personal developmental needs of children and youth. Fortunately, through project-based, experiential, child-directed learning activities, after-school programs are optimally suited to provide opportunities to develop precisely these "new basic skills" in young people.

Incorporating Technology into After-School

Due to the growing interest in using computers and related technology in after-school programs, this guide contains one entire chapter and numerous sidebars devoted to the subject. The overarching recommendation is that technology be integrated into a program's larger learning goals, not be a separate, stand-alone activity or an end to itself. This approach is informed by the work of the YouthLearn Initiative at Education Development Center (EDC). [3]

"Teaching how to create a web page or use a drawing program should be part of a project on building language or math skills, not an end in itself. Kids need to understand that technology is just another tool for learning and communication, just like a book or a pencil."

— *From the YouthLearn Initiative at EDC*

---

[3] For more information about the YouthLearn Initiative, visit their website at: www.youthlearn.org. *The YouthLearn Guide: A Creative Approach to Working with Youth and Technology*, ©Education Development Center, Inc., 2001, provides specific and detailed instruction on ways to incorporate technology-rich activities into out-of-school-time programs.

Using What We Know About Learning

Learning is a step-by-step process of accumulating, constructing and understanding knowledge gained by being physically and socially active and involved in the world, over the course of a lifetime. Learning is also a cycle, because the phases repeat themselves as learning deepens over time. Learning is also shaped by the cultural, familial and biological realities the learner brings with them to the process.[4]

Increased public concern about students' academic performance coincides with a growing recognition of the importance of combating alienation, drug use and violence among young people by focusing on other aspects of their development. Research has made clear that social and emotional variables are critically important to children's engagement, motivation and attachment to school.

Children who are afraid, anxious, unable to manage their emotions or recognize and appreciate other people's perspectives are severely impaired in their ability to perform well in school or develop to their fullest potential.[5] Thus, there is an emerging consensus that a key to meeting both academic and social goals for children and youth is by attending to their "social and emotional learning" needs.

Learning Styles

Children, like adults, learn in different ways. Some people learn best by watching others, and some learn best by being able to talk or write or draw about a particular subject. Styles of learning can also change depending on the task at hand. It is important to think about different learning styles when planning an after-school curriculum and to pay attention to these differences when working with children and youth.

---

[4] For more information about how learning theory can shape after-school and youth programming, see: Georgia Hall, Nicole Yohalem, Joel Tolman and Alicia Wilson, "How After-School Programs Can Most Effectively Promote Positive Youth Development as a Support to Academic Achievement," A Report Commissioned by the Boston After-School for All Partnership," National Institute on Out-of-School Time, 2003. http://www.niost.org/WCW3.pdf

[5] Adapted from: "Guidelines for Social and Emotional Learning: Quality Programs for School and Life Success," Collaborative for Academic, Social and Emotional Learning (CASEL), July 2002. www.casel.org/downloads/Safe%20and%20Sound/2A_Guidelines.pdf

One way researchers think about learning styles is by breaking learners down into three basic types: visual, auditory and kinesthetic (or sensory) learners.

- **Visual Learners** relate most effectively to written information, notes, diagrams and pictures. Visual learners will tend to be most effective in written communication or symbol manipulation, e.g. math and art. Visual learners make up about 65 percent of the population.

- **Auditory Learners** relate most effectively to the spoken word. Often written information will have little meaning until it has been heard. Auditory learners may be accomplished speakers. Auditory learners make up about 30 percent of the population.

- **Kinesthetic (or Sensory) Learners** learn most effectively through touch and movement and they learn skills best by imitation and practice. Predominantly kinesthetic learners can have great difficulty in traditional school settings since most information is not normally presented in a way that suits their learning style. Kinesthetic learners make up about 5 percent of the population.

Another way to think about learning styles is presented in the following diagram that draws on research on human intelligence and learning to describe four types of learners:

Links to Learning: *A Curriculum Planning Guide for After-School Programs*

Four Learning Styles[6]

ST Sensing-Thinking (ST) or Master Learner

PREFERS TO LEARN BY:

- seeing tangible results
- practicing what he has learned
- following directions one step at a time
- being active rather than passive
- knowing exactly what is expected of her, how well the task must be done and why

LEARNS BEST FROM:

- drill
- demonstration
- practice
- hands-on experience

LIKES:

- doing things that have immediate, practical use
- being acknowledged for thoroughness and detail
- praise for prompt and complete work
- immediate feedback (rewards, privileges, etc.)

DISLIKES:

- completing tasks for which there are no practical uses
- activities that require imagination and intuition
- activities with complex directions
- open-ended activities without closure or pay-off
- activities that focus on feelings or other intangible results

NT Intuitive-Thinking (NT) or Understanding Learner

PREFERS TO LEARN BY:

- studying about ideas and how things are related
- planning and carrying out a project of his own making and interest
- arguing or debating a point based on logical analysis
- problem solving that requires collecting, organizing and evaluating data

LEARNS BEST FROM:

- lectures
- reading
- logical discussions and debates
- projects of personal interest

LIKES:

- time to plan and organize her work
- working independently or with other intuitive-thinking types
- working with ideas and things that challenge him to think, to explore, to master

DISLIKES:

- routine or rote assignments
- memorization
- concern for details
- rigid rules and predetermined procedures

SF Sensing-Feeling (SF) or Interpersonal Learner

PREFERS TO LEARN BY:

- studying about things that directly affect people's lives rather than impersonal facts or theories
- receiving personal attention and encouragement from his teachers
- being part of a team - collaborating with other students
- activities that help her learn about herself and how she feels about things

LEARNS BEST FROM:

- group experiences and projects
- loving attention
- personal expression and personal encounters
- role playing

LIKES:

- receiving personal attention and encouragement
- opportunities to be helpful in class
- personal feedback
- sharing personal feelings and experiences with others

DISLIKES:

- long periods of working alone silently
- emphasis on factual detail
- highly competitive games where someone loses
- detailed and demanding routines

NF Intuitive-Feeling (NF) or Self-Expressive Learner

PREFERS TO LEARN BY:

- being creative and using his imagination
- planning and organizing her work in her own creative ways
- working on a number of things at one time
- searching for alternative solutions to problems beyond those normally considered
- discussing real problems and looking for real solutions

LEARNS BEST FROM:

- creative and artistic activities
- open-ended discussions of personal and social values
- activities that enlighten and enhance – myths, human achievement, dramas, etc.

LIKES:

- contemplation
- being able to learn through discovery
- opportunity to plan and pursue his own interests
- recognition for personal insights and discoveries

DISLIKES:

- too much attention to detail
- facts, memorization, rote learning
- tasks with predetermined correct answers
- detailed and demanding routines

[6] Adapted from: Silver, Harvey F., Richard W. Strong, and Matthew J. Perini. *So Each May Learn: Integrating Learning Styles and Multiple Intelligences.* Alexandria, VA: Association for Supervision and Curriculum Development. 2000.

Section 2

In addition to different learning styles, research on motivation has taught us which characteristics improve or detract from children's interest in learning. In general, the more choices children and youth have about what they learn and how they learn it, the more relevant it is to their lives and the more active they are in the learning process, the more motivated and engaged they will be.

Factors That Influence Attention for Learning

Increase Intrinsic Motivation (Hook Attention for 10-90 minutes)		Increase Apathy and Resentment (Hook attention for 10 minutes or less)
Choices	Vs.	**Required**
▪ provide choices regarding: content, timing, work partners, projects, process, environment and resources		▪ directed 100 percent ▪ no student input ▪ resources restricted ▪ working alone
Relevant	Vs.	**Irrelevant**
▪ make it personal: relate to family, neighborhood, city, life stages, love, health, etc.		▪ impersonal, out of context, of unclear use, or done only to pass a test
Active	Vs.	**Passive**
▪ make it emotional and energetic ▪ make it physical ▪ use learner-imposed deadlines and peer pressure		▪ disconnected from the real world ▪ low interaction: lecture, seatwork, or video

To increase engagement and motivation, effective programs strive to make their activities "child-centered," that is, structured around the children's natural curiosity rather than around topics deemed important by grown-ups.[8] By building on children's interests, staff can capitalize on children and youth's inherent motivation to teach them skills they need in order to understand or master something they care about. Among the differences between traditional classrooms and "child-centered" ones are the following:

---

[7] Jensen, Eric. *Teaching with the Brain in Mind*, Alexandria, VA: Association for Supervision and Curriculum Development. 1998.

[8] Child-centered teaching discussion adapted from: Carter, Margie and Deb Curtis. *Reflecting Children's Lives: A Handbook for Planning Child Centered Curriculum*, St. Paul, MN: Red Leaf Press. 1996.

Traditional Approaches	Child-Centered Approach
Teacher-directed curriculum themes overshadow or hide children's interests. Look-alike products are displayed on the bulletin boards with no sign of individual children's imaginations or interests.	Staff use children's ideas as the basis for curriculum planning. Planning involves an introduction of materials and interactions to stimulate the emergence of the children's ideas.
Teachers base their plans on traditional school topics, popular culture, holidays and pre-packaged seasonal curriculum theme books. Curriculum plans are pulled from files and activity books and are repeated on an annual basis.	Staff members share their own passions, interests and questions, which may serve as another source to stimulate children's interests and develop the curriculum.
Teacher planning is focused only on the entire group, not the individuals within that group, neglecting to make regular changes to the environment in accordance with specific children's needs/abilities/interests.	Staff plans the environment as the basis for the curriculum, which is child-centered and reflects the children's interests and lives. Materials are in good condition, interesting and organized with attention to aesthetics.
Teachers tend to ignore most non-disruptive child-initiated play. Instead, they do housekeeping and record keeping tasks during "free choice" time.	Staff members observe individual children and the themes of their physical, cognitive, social and emotional development. They make note of the children's questions, skills and frustrations and use them in lesson planning.

Guidelines for Transforming to a Child-Centered Approach

Step One: Set the Stage and Allow Time

Plan the environment. Organize the space and material to allow for choices and possibilities.

Step Two: Open the Space
Let the Children Combine Different Areas

Avoid being too rigid with rules that require manipulatives to remain in certain areas. Stock your room with an ample supply of open-ended materials.

Step Three: Avoid Interrupting Significant Play

Enable children to become truly absorbed in activities of their choosing. When not interrupted, children are able to sustain complex, cooperative play and language for longer periods of time.

Step Four: Keep the Clean-up Options Open

Ensure the play episode has reached a natural conclusion before requesting that a child clean up. What may look like a mess may be a child's imagination in full bloom.

Step Five: Refer Children to Each Other

Build a learning community. Children need to see themselves as competent and resourceful. Whenever possible, let children offer assistance to one another. Model and coach supportive interactions.

Step Six: Observe Consciously

Observe individual children and the themes of their physical, cognitive, social and emotional development. Make note of the children's questions, skills and frustrations and engage with them or plan activities that aid their understanding and development.

To be most effective, after-school programs should adopt a child-centered approach in their curriculum planning, incorporating knowledge of learning styles and research on motivation.

Using What We Know About Child Development

Probably no other industry has applied knowledge of child and youth development better than the clothing industry. Sizes, styles, materials, decoration and construction details are all informed with knowledge of human development related to weight, height, preferences, trends, maturational issues and cultural expectations. Decisions whether to use buttons, zippers or Velcro™ are based on knowing a lot about what children can and cannot do, as well as what they will or will not do at particular ages. Similar thought must go into choosing and implementing activities for children and youth in after-school programs.

Age and Development

Age and development are not synonymous. Development for an individual is a function of the realities of nature and nurture, life experiences, overall personal, physical, emotional and social health, and quality of life in general. Knowing general developmental characteristics associated with different ages, however, can help staff determine what kinds of experiences are best for children and youth and can help them anticipate what may occur during certain activities. Finally, knowing these developmental characteristics can help staff effectively introduce, motivate, encourage and direct children and youth.

Children 6 - 10

In order for staff to understand how best to serve children, it is important that they understand where young children are in their development. The following characteristics are general ones for this age group.

Children's Characteristics (Ages 6-10)	Adult Roles
▪ The youngest children in this age group are often (but not always) very busy, sloppy, erratic and in a rush to complete a task. As they get older, their interest in being both neat and correct grows.	▪ Adults can set examples and model desirable behavior. Be patient with this phase in what is really a process.
▪ Having and keeping friends becomes important. Children often have "best" friends or partners of choice.	▪ Adults can encourage friends to sit together, play together, have snack together and work at resolving issues that threaten their friendships.
▪ Children learn new things and need to constantly replace old ways of thinking with new ways. Leaving the familiar for new untried ways is difficult for some.	▪ Adults can help children recall how successful they have been in the past during unfamiliar experiences and how normal it is to be unsure about alternative ways of thinking about something.
▪ Children are generally more eager to learn, more curious, more enthusiastic and more imaginative at this age than at any other time in their lives.	▪ Adults can use these qualities to regularly introduce many new experiences to children.
▪ Children begin to apply logic to solving problems and get good at using numbers, letters and words.	▪ Adults can provide children with lots of guidance and opportunities to solve problems; offer games that use numbers, letters and words to support their learning.
▪ Children need routine and consistency from adults in their lives.	▪ With routine and consistency children do not have to worry or wonder what comes next or what behavior is expected. Flexibility is important, however.
▪ Discovering things and inventing are favorite activities.	▪ Adults can ask children to make or design things that solve real and immediate problems in the program.
▪ Take-apart and put-together activities are popular.	▪ Adults serve this interest when they bring in items that can safely be taken apart. Encourage the parts to be used in interesting ways.
▪ Writing can be a favored activity especially when it helps children get something they want or need.	▪ Labeling, pen-pal writing, shopping lists, program posters are all great writing experiences with potential payoffs.
▪ Children enjoy math if it is connected to and supports what they are invested in.	▪ Adults can use games, cooking activities and problem solving to reinforce math skills.
▪ Children are naturally curious about and generally highly motivated to use technology for learning.	▪ Adults can facilitate the constructive use of technology through child-directed, project-based learning activities.
▪ Science is seen by children as a way to explain the world they are becoming more and more curious about.	▪ Adults can read up on the scientific issues children show interest in.

Youth 11 - 14

In order for staff to understand how best to serve this age group, it is important to understand where young adolescents are in their development. The following characteristics are general ones for this age group.

Youth's Characteristics (Ages 11-14)	Adult Roles
▪ Begin to develop more personal self-awareness concerning the physical, social and emotional changes that are rapidly occurring for them.	▪ Adults need to be sensitive and patient as youth struggle with these changes.
▪ Begin to challenge their own ideas about how they think the world works, as well as challenging the adult rules they used to live by without question.	▪ Although challenge may appear to be personally directed, adults must remember the challenge is about the issue, not the adult.
▪ May begin to show skill in certain content and ability areas.	▪ Adults can show interest in these areas and encourage youth to build on potential career directions.
▪ Youth copy their peers in how to behave, how to dress, what to admire, etc. They put lots of energy into developing and perfecting their own sense of self or identity. Often self-absorbed, but eager to be in the company of their friends.	▪ Adults need to help youth differentiate between when it's appropriate or acceptable to "follow" and when they need to pull back from a group because certain behavior is unwise.
▪ Youth want to talk to adults but don't always know how. Older youth enjoy relationships with caring adults.	▪ Adults who are skilled listeners are highly prized by youth. Practice good listening skills by listening more than speaking.
▪ Youth have a strong desire for independence, especially from the constraints that are more typical of "little kids."	▪ Don't eliminate rules; have rules that match older children's abilities to be responsible. Provide spaces, activities and privileges to youth that are different from those available to younger children.
▪ Youth like to have their ideas solicited by adults rather than volunteering them.	▪ Provide positive recognition as youth attempt to assume more mature behavior.
▪ Youth generally enjoy helping younger children, being part of planning for them, establishing rules associated with the plans and assuming leadership.	▪ Adults can strive to include youth in programs for young children.
▪ Fairness in all things is a guiding principle in young teens' lives. They are quite alert and sensitive to adult behavior that is perceived as unfair.	▪ Adults must be consistent and fair in their interactions, help and discipline.
▪ Children and youth depart from playing together and often gather in all-girl or all-boy groups. Thirteen is thought to be the year with the greatest amount of boy/girl developmental differences. Girls at this age often take interest in older boys.	▪ Adults need to be sensitive to these shifts.

Links to Learning: *A Curriculum Planning Guide for After-School Programs*

Resiliency and Asset Development

It is important to understand how learning happens and the stages and phases of development. However, if children and youth don't have certain personal and social "assets" – including resiliency – learning and overall development will be put at risk.

What is resiliency? Resiliency is the ability to recover or adapt in the face of adversity. For young people who have one or more known risk factors – characteristics or experiences that can compromise their optimal development – resiliency is critically important.

Why are we concerned about risk factors? The presence of risk factors limits a child's ability to perform in school and develop the emotional and social competence to successfully transition through adolescence into adulthood. There is a 30-year body of knowledge about how to build protective factors that will help children and youth adapt to risks, make good decisions and ultimately overcome the challenges they face. The following chart identifies key factors that put children's development at risk. It also identifies "protective factors" that research has shown make children less susceptible to these risks or more "resilient."[9]

Factors	Risk Factors	Protective Factors
Individual/ Constitutional	Neuro-developmental delay Difficult temperament	Higher cognitive functioning Easy temperament Psycho-physiological health (e.g. self-confidence)
Family	Poverty, substance abuse, abusive parenting	Nurturing and supportive Literate Organized and predictable
Neighborhood	Community violence High levels of mobility	Safe and stable Accessible services
Schools and Peers	Poor quality school Negative encounters with teachers and/or peers	Good quality preschool Positive relationships with staff and peers

While there is often little that after-school programs can do to affect individual or family risk factors, there is much that programs can do to impact the protective factors provided by neighborhood and school/peers. By providing safe, stable and accessible services and by facilitating positive relationships with staff and peers, after-school programs can help at-risk children and youth immensely.

The Search Institute's Healthy Communities, Healthy Youth Initiative has researched and disseminated a framework of "40 Developmental Assets" that help children and youth grow up resilient, healthy, caring and responsible.[10] These assets are clustered under categories of both internal and external assets and include the need for:

- Support
- Empowerment
- Boundaries and Expectations
- Constructive Uses of Time
- Commitment to Learning
- Positive Values and Social Competencies

---

[9] Hawkins, D.J. and R.F. Catalano, *Communities That Care Prevention Strategies: A Research Guide to What Works*. Developmental Research and Programs. 1996.

[10] See Section 4 for a complete list of The Search Institute's 40 Developmental Assets.

By examining these developmental assets and using them to inform activity choices, programs can help children and youth build the protective factors they need to succeed.

How "Developmental Assets" Can Inform Program Activities[11]

Asset #25: Commitment to Learning – Reading For Pleasure: Children and caring adults read and read together for at least 30 minutes a day. Children also enjoy reading or looking at books or magazines on their own.

In our environment, we can:
a. provide a caring adult to read to interested children during our programs
b. provide a variety of developmentally and culturally appropriate books for children to read
c. provide separate listening and reading areas, with books on tape
d. provide a comfy area for reading
e. ensure the space is enriched with lots of rich print
f. use the school's library

In our relationships, we can:
a. read to children and speak with children often
b. ask children to read to us and to younger children
c. ask children to tell us about their favorite books

In our experiences, we can:
a. take field trips to the library
b. take children to senior centers to read to senior citizens
c. organize book clubs
d. participate in school book fairs
e. organize a newsletter club
f. encourage teens to read to children

---

[11] Adapted from: Mike Ashcraft, "Assets Ideas," Albuquerque, NM. 2000.

Discussion Questions for Section Two

1. Think about something you know how to do very well. It could be knitting a sweater, driving a car, pounding a nail, telling a joke or tying your shoelaces. Describe how you learned it. Did someone teach you how to do it? Did you watch someone else do it and try to imitate or replicate? Would you describe your learning as a process with stages or steps, or some other way?

2. How would you characterize your own learning style? Give some examples.

3. Describe how you help others learn something. Are your methods different depending on whom you are helping and what you are helping them to learn?

4. Think about your own "teachers" in a broad sense, individuals you encountered in a school setting, but also those who helped you learn something in non-academic settings. Who were some of your favorite teachers (or adults)? Why did you like them so much? What were their appealing characteristics? How did they get you interested in trying new activities, striving to learn or be your best?

5. What characteristics of "good teachers" come up most often in the group discussion? What are the characteristics of least favorite teachers?

6. Among the characteristics of good teachers, which ones do you believe others would note in watching you in your after-school work? What would you most like to improve in your work with children and youth? Generate a list for yourself and share with the group one of the skills you'd like to work on.

NOTES

Section Three:

Curriculum Planning Basics

Developing a Mission

Goals and Objectives

Choosing Activities
- Types of Activities
- Attending to Children and Youth's Needs and Interests

Developing an Activity Plan
- Preparing for Activities
- Engaging Children and Youth

Scheduling
- Daily, Weekly, Monthly and Yearly Scheduling
- Balancing the Schedule

Evaluation
- Why Evaluate?
- What to Assess?
- Linking Evaluation to Goals
- Evaluation Resources

Additional Curriculum Planning Resources

Section 3

NOTES

Section Three
Curriculum Planning Basics

Your mission will inform decisions about all dimensions of the program and determine what occurs at your site on a day-to-day basis.

Developing a Mission

Every program needs a mission statement – a philosophy or rationale explaining the purpose of the program. The mission (also sometimes called the "vision") shapes the program and guides decision making. The mission statement is built on the desired developmental or learning outcomes for the children and youth attending the program.

A strong mission statement for an after-school program reveals why children and youth should spend time at the program, what they should be doing there, and what they should be learning there. In determining your program mission, ask: "What do we want for our children? What kinds of experiences are important for them to have?"

There are many reasons why children and youth attend after-school programs and they form the backbone of most program missions. Some reasons are:

- To provide families with a safe environment for children and youth to spend the hours which extend beyond the school day.

- To provide children and youth with opportunities and experiences not typically found during the school day.

- To provide children and youth with opportunities to develop artistically, physically and/or socially.

- To provide children and youth opportunities for personal growth through involvement in adventure learning or community service projects.

- To provide children and youth with a safe, predicable setting in which to develop the academic skills needed to do well in school or on achievement tests.

- To help children and youth develop career prospects by learning the skills of a profession or through opportunities to participate in the profession.

The organization uses the power of the mission to bring people together and direct their energies to a common purpose.
— Frances Hesselbein, Drucker Foundation for Non-Profit Management

In considering the mission for your program, it may be useful to think about what kinds of knowledge you want children and youth in your care to gain. The following ways to categorize knowledge may be helpful to think about when articulating the mission for your program or selecting activities.

Personal-Emotional Knowledge - Information and understanding concerning one's self.

Social-Relational Knowledge - Information about and skills relating to people, how to get along with them, and how and why they behave in the ways they do.

Physical Knowledge - Information about and skill in using one's body.

Academic Knowledge - Information and skills in reading, writing, math, science, languages, history, etc.

The following are sample after-school mission statements that may help you think about, define or refine your mission:

- To offer many ways for young adolescents to feel competent, to achieve and to develop their individual potential.

- To provide a warm and enriching environment for kindergarten through sixth grade students. Our philosophy is one of providing structure with room for individual choice.

- To help children and youth build a healthy spirit, mind, and body.[12]

- To serve children and youth.

- To provide children and youth of working parents with a safe, home-like atmosphere.

- To meet the needs of the local community by offering parents a place for their children and youth to be supervised in a quality after-school recreational and enrichment program.

Goals and Objectives

Goal statements break your mission down into specific parts reflecting what you want to achieve.[13] Objectives are statements of how you will achieve your goals and may include specific activities or strategies. Objectives must be specific and contain measurable outcomes. Objectives will also help you articulate the reasons why you chose specific activities or adopted particular strategies. For example, if one of your objectives is to "help children and youth develop new skills and interests," that objective will shape the breadth and depth of your program, spurring you to offer activities that enhance children's physical, social, intellectual, artistic and emotional development. It might also explain why project-based or social-competence activities form a large part of your curriculum.

---

[12] The mission of the YMCA of the USA.

[13] The following discussion of goals and objectives is adapted from the "School of the 21st Century Implementation Manual," Yale University, 1998, www.yale.edu/21C, and "A Guide to Continuous Improvement Management (CIM) for 21st Century Community Learning Centers," U.S. Department of Education, February 1999. www.ed.gov/offices/OUS/PES/21cent/cim226.pdf

When setting objectives, it is important to keep coming back to the questions. "How will we know if we have succeeded? What are the expected outcomes?" Thinking through the expected outcomes for each objective will help you figure out how to measure success and will help you with evaluation and program improvement efforts in the long run.

Example:

Mission: Our program will provide a unique learning environment that will stimulate children's curiosity while reinforcing essential academic learning.

Goal: To increase student motivation and interest in academic subject matter.

Objective: Our program will provide at least one activity focused on a core school subject area to at least 300 different children over the next three years and each child will participate in the activity for at least half the possible time.

Choosing Activities

Once you have clearly defined your program's mission and have set your goals and objectives, you are ready to begin thinking about activities. Choosing activities should be based on six core concepts:

- The mission, goals and objectives of the program and the expected outcomes for children

- Attention to children's needs and interests

- An understanding of how children learn and develop

- The limits and assets of the program's space and resources

- The group leaders' teaching styles and strengths

- The daily schedule of the program

You can find activity ideas in guides, workshops or by talking to other people who work with children and youth. You will need to develop your own definition for what a "good activity" is. For example, you might ask yourself:

- Does it meet my goals and objectives?

- Is it relevant to the children and youth I work with?

- Is it fun?

- Is it consistent with school-age best practices?[14]

---

[14] See Section 4 for more on linking activities to quality standards.

After implementing activities developed by others, you can begin to develop your own. Sometimes your first original activity is a simple variation of someone else's idea. Your version will be very much shaped by your personal experiences and strengths and by the children and youth you work with, as well as your program objectives and hoped-for child outcomes. As described in Section 5, selecting a theme can make it easier to choose and organize activities.

What are "After-School Appropriate" Activities?

After-school appropriate activities support literacy development, problem-solving skills, scientific and artistic discovery and project-based learning opportunities. They are activities done in a materials-rich, experientially-based program which enhances, supplements and complements the learning that occurs in the rest of a child's life.

Types of Activities

There are numerous types of activities in any after-school program. Some activities are brief and only occur once – a brainteaser, an icebreaker or a guest visitor. Some activities span the course of many days – a theater production or a multi-step art project. Some are frequently repeated – sports, songs, games, crafts. Some activities fit within a theme developed by the program (e.g. animals, magnets, or mirrors). Complex activities that last many days are sometimes called "project-based activities." Project-based activities have many of the attractive qualities of play – in that they are fun for children – but they provide more intentional and planned learning experiences. *(See Section 5 for a lengthy discussion of theme-and project-based activities.)* In the course of any given day, a program will have time for many different types of activities.

Finding Activities on the Internet

The Internet is a logical place to turn for inspiration for creating activity plans and for the plans themselves. Be prepared though – you may have to read through a lot of lesson plans on the Internet to find ones that are well-written, challenging and interesting. Here are a few things to keep in mind as you look around:

- **Know the audience.** Determine whom the lesson plans were written for. What is the intended or assumed age of children, prerequisite knowledge, prerequisite skills, availability of resources, and cultural context?

- **Be critical.** When you encounter a lesson plan that is appropriate and interesting, you may have to adapt it to suit the individual and group needs of your children. Note the source of any materials used and trace it to a point where you can find more information on the author or organization.

- **Use the tools to get more information.** If a site is active, you may be able to contact the person who wrote or compiled the materials. Sending a question or request for more information may bring new leads on good materials, sources of materials, or other people interested in the same areas of information.

- **Be a scavenger.** Rather than looking for a whole complete lesson or project, you may want to do a broader search on a theme, topic or question. A quick search on the Web, or posting a question on an email list, can yield direct information or useful recommendations that might spark an idea, provide a model or give directions on how to do or find something.

- From the YouthLearn Initiative at EDC

Attending to Children and Youth's Needs and Interests

Making programs "child-centered" is one of the best ways to ensure that children and youth are engaged and able to learn. One of the best ways to engage them is to involve them in the program planning. You can do this in a variety of ways.

1. Talk with children and youth about the activities they like to do the most. Ask:

   - What are your favorite things to do?

   - What do we do now in the program that you enjoy?

   - What could we do more of?

   - What have you always wished you could learn about?

   - What do other children and youth say they like to do in after-school programs?

2. Make suggestions based on what you know about the children. Younger children may need more adult suggestions/input than older children.

3. Start with what children know and build on it. For example, if you have picked a theme of "Parks," the children might know that there are statues of famous people located in parks around the program. Ask if they know anything about those people and the role they played in the history of the city. Or, they may be able to tell you the names of animals found in the parks but know very little about what they eat, where they spend their time during the day, or how close you can get to them before they run or fly away. Either or both of these topics could set you off on a series of exciting child-centered activities or projects.

Developing an Activity Plan

Every program's activity plans may look different, but might include most of the following components (see Appendix B for a template):

Title:
Every learning activity needs a title to help distinguish it from others.

Description:
Provide a brief description of the activity.

Objectives:
When planning any activity refer back to your program's goals and objectives and determine which objective(s) this activity relates to best. Consider how the activity links both to learning benchmarks and quality standards (see Section 4).

Intended Outcomes:
The objective is always connected to an intended outcome – what the planner hopes will be experienced or learned once the activity is finished.

Special Materials & Tools:
Some activities may be purely verbal or physical so no raw materials or tools may be needed. However, some activities require unusual materials or tools that are not part of the routine supplies.

Space Requirements:
Suggestions concerning the kind of work surface; the amount of floor area or table area needed; or the characteristics of the space or environment that are needed to support the activities to happen there.

Age/Group Size:
What age(s) is this activity appropriate for and/or what skills must they possess? How big or small can or must the group be for the activity to work well?

The Activity:
Describe the various phases or components of the activity including how to introduce the activity. At the outset, either detail the rules for involvement in the activity, or introduce the participants to what will be done, experienced or learned while participating in the activity. This is a critical component of all activities and can "make or break" their ultimate success.

Incorporating Technology:
Describe ways to incorporate computers or other technology into the project either through an extension or by varying the approach.

Extensions and Continuations:
An activity can occur once and never be done again. Or it can be repeated often. Some activities can be modified and then repeated. Other activities can lead to related activities. For example, a trip to the zoo can lead to drawing the animals that were seen, which can lead to painting a hallway "zoo" mural.

Conclusions/Reflections:

As each activity finishes, learners can be asked to reflect on the activity and what occurred during it. Thoughts, feelings, a sense of what was enjoyed or learned, what to do differently next time, can all be shared with other participants. This becomes a nice way to assess, as well as to bring closure to an event.

Documentation:

Photographs, audio and videotapes, the art products created, any written materials including notes, are all examples of documents which record individual learning, as well as create a record of the history of participation and preserve the activity experience.

Preparing for Activities

It is one thing to select high-quality activities for children and youth and be able to say why you chose them; however, it is another thing to be able to introduce and facilitate an activity well. Effective facilitation takes skill, practice and insight. Implementation of any activity must be preceded with a lot of planning and preparation.

Recall the learning cycle

- In each learning experience, adults intentionally move the children and youth through the learning cycle phases of awareness, exploration, inquiry and utilization. The beginning of any activity should help children and youth develop awareness. This opening will serve to get them excited about what else will happen in the activity, alert them to the content they will be learning about, remind them of the expectations and invite them into planning the experience. In the course of an activity, adults instruct when necessary, encourage the child to do things for themselves, suggest ideas to try out, ensure proper use of materials, reward where appropriate, listen to children and model the behaviors most hoped for in the learners.

The Learning Cycle

- *Awareness/Exposure* A recognition that phenomenon, objects, concepts and events exist. **Example:** Adult puts out a glue stick, an item the learner has never seen or used before.

- *Exploration/Play/Instruct* The activity in which a learner finds out about what they have been exposed to in as many ways as there are to find out about things. **Example:** Learner actively tries to figure out what a glue stick is, how it opens, how it gets dispensed, how it smells. May ask adult or peer about it.

- *Inquire/Compare* The learner relates what new information s/he has gained to what s/he already knew. At this point learners may revise their prior understanding, or they may reject the new information as useless or unrelated to anything already understood. **Example:** The learner may watch others use the glue stick on paper to compare their techniques. May ask others for their opinions.

- *Utilization/Practice* Learners apply their understanding of events, objects, or concepts to solve problems or understand what they see or hear. **Example:** The learner uses the glue stick to see if it will stick pieces of wood together.

Set the stage

- Gather the resources, tools, materials and reference materials you need to support the chosen activities. Having adequate supplies is a vital part of all after-school program activities. One of the best ways to anticipate what will be needed is to try each activity before doing it with the children. Think about additional materials that might be important to have on hand given your knowledge about what various children and youth are interested in and the new directions they may want to go with an activity.

- Select a space that is safe, appropriate to the nature of the activity, provides the necessary amount of space to accommodate the activity at its fullest, is roomy enough for the largest number of children involved and allows, if necessary, for the project to exist for a number of days.

- Talk it up; show enthusiasm. Encourage other adults to be curious and interested in what the children will be doing.

Create groups that work well together

- Think about how children in your program work together. If they generally work well together, let them self-select into the groups they want to work in. If some children have a history of not working well with others, make sure they are either in separate groups or have adequate adult supervision not to derail the activity. In creating groups, mix ability levels, genders and age levels wherever possible.

Plan the time

- The schedule should allow sufficient time. Inadequate time that doesn't allow children to get into the project at some depth can be frustrating and may imply, in the child's mind, that the project is not important, producing a superficial commitment. Groups may need more time than individuals, since there is a need to share materials and tools, collaborate and carry on discussions.

Create a positive climate

- Climate affects how people behave and feel. A supportive learning environment is physically, culturally, emotionally and intellectually safe. That means it is okay to express ideas, even if they are different from the majority; it is okay to ask for help from adults and peers; and it is okay to be different. In a supportive environment everyone is expected to be polite and respectful. The tools, materials and environment are safe and appropriate for the ages using them. Adults show interest in what children are doing and are available to help when needed. A variety of cultures are represented in the staff or invited guests, books, audio-visuals, posters and literature chosen to accompany an activity. If any of these qualities are missing, children and youth may not feel comfortable fully participating in an experience.

Engaging Children and Youth

Having chosen, planned and prepared for an activity, now it is time to consider how to introduce the activity and get children and youth to want to participate. Here are some implementation tips and ideas:

Affirm, Share, and Celebrate

Have children affirm, share and celebrate what they already know about the concepts and knowledge that are part of the activity they are about to try. People like to share what they know and it's important for adults to have a sense at the outset of what the group already knows. In this way they can adjust the activity or define leadership opportunities for knowledgeable participants.

Motivate

You are creating an experience tailored to what you feel is best for the group, the site and the schedule to allow children and youth to learn something or provide them with a new experience. Motivation techniques:

- Provide directions/example (show them how to do/make something); or

- Challenge the children and youth (to find a better solution on their own); or

- Invite open exploration (of an idea or material) in which there may be several solutions/uses.

Involve Children and Youth in Creating a Plan

Though you have already created an activity plan that clarified the learning goals of this activity, you also want to engage the children in planning for the activity, inviting them to bring their own interests, questions and thoughts to bear. Through discussion or brainstorming, help the children and youth create a plan for how best to approach the activity, implement the directions, meet the challenge, or study the idea. For project-based activities, it is especially important to encourage the children to "think before they leap," develop a strategy, then implement it. Impulsive, spontaneous solutions not talked out in a whole group format often include only the aggressive participants and leave the more reflective participants out of the activity unsure of how to participate in a meaningful way.

Implement the Group's Ideas

Once the group has a plan, invite the children to implement it. Here the collective ideas of all members of the group are reflected and each participant feels like s/he is part of the plan. Conclude the study/activity by having the children and youth share what occurred and what they learned. Sharing what was learned is one of the best ways to gauge and reinforce your program's learning objectives. Public forums for sharing can also be a way to keep parents and the community informed about the learning that is happening in your program.

Scheduling

Planning for activities – or long-term projects that may include several activities – must take place within the context of overall planning for the program. The following are a few tools to help with daily, weekly, monthly and yearly scheduling.

Daily, Weekly, Monthly and Yearly Scheduling

Daily Schedule

Though each program is unique, a program's daily schedule should contain most of the following general components:

Arrival, Transition and Free Time
 Crafts, table games, outdoor play, conversation, clean up

Snack
 Healthy choices, opportunities both to prepare and to eat food

Meeting
 Chance to meet as a group, set expectations, plan, go over questions, brainstorm or address problems

Activity Choices (large groups and small, short term and long term)
 - Art projects: drama/music/dance/painting/drawing/sculpture
 - Science or math problem-solving: experiments, construction, exploration, nature walks, calculations
 - Literacy: reading, writing, communication
 - Fitness and health: exercise, nutrition
 - Technology: media production, research, communication, documentation

Outdoor games/activities
 - Group sports
 - Individual skills/fitness
 - Nature/environment

Homework Support
 Quiet space, tutoring assistance

Week-at-a-Glance by Activity Type

This weekly planning tool focuses on daily activity areas. Insert specific activities into the schedule and post a completed plan. Use the plan to set up and document the experiences the program creates for children and youth.

	Monday	Tuesday	Wednesday	Thursday	Friday
Arrival	Art activity Table games Computer activity Make snack	Art activity Literacy activity Table games Make snack	Art activity Literacy activity Science activity Make snack	Art activity Table games Computer activity Make snack	Science activity Table games Math games Make snack
Snack	Pizza bagels Juice	Crackers, cheese Juice	Apples, grapes Banana smoothies	Nachos Water	Carrot, celery and hummus Juice
Home-work Support	Homework Station: Tutor assistance	Homework Station: Tutor assistance	Homework Station: Tutor assistance	Homework Station: Tutor assistance	Homework Station: Tutor assistance
Large group activity	Reading and discussion	Art project	Math games	Writing activity	Trust game
Group projects (large or small groups)	Math projects	Science/ Technology activity	Neighborhood project planning	Neighborhood project implementation	Music/Theater/ Dance
Outdoor games/ activities	Softball	All Hands on Deck	Volleyball	4 Square, jump rope, hopscotch	Kids' choice
Other					

Section 3

Week-at-a-Glance by Core Content Areas

This weekly planning chart can help you check that your program is balanced and addressing all the core content areas that you have selected. How frequently a particular type of activity is offered is based on your program mission, objectives and desired outcomes.

	Monday	Tuesday	Wednesday	Thursday	Friday
Literacy (daily)	Large group: reading and discussion	Arrival: literacy activity	Arrival: literacy activity	Large group: writing activity	Group project: music/theater/ dance
Arts (daily)	Arrival: art activity	Arrival: art activity Large group: art project	Arrival: art activity	Arrival: art activity	Group project: music/theater/ dance
Health & Fitness (daily)	Outdoor games and activities	Outdoor games and activities	Outdoor games and activities	Outdoor games and activities	Outdoor games and activities
Math (3x/week)	Group project: math project		Large group: math games		Arrival: math games
Science (2-3x/week)		Group Project: science/ technology	Arrival: science activity		Arrival: science activity
Technology (2-3x/week)	Arrival: computer activity project	Group project: science/ technology		Arrival: computer activity	
Social-Competence (2x/week)			Large group: neighborhood project planning	Large group: neighborhood project implementation	Large group: game
Other					

Links to Learning: *A Curriculum Planning Guide for After-School Programs*

Daily, Weekly, Monthly and Yearly Planning Chart

This form can help you think broadly about your program, looking at weekly, monthly and yearly activities to ensure that the curriculum is balanced over time.

Components of an After-School Program: A Planning Guide and Checklist

Daily	Monday	Tuesday	Wednesday	Thursday	Friday
Recreation/Play					
Homework Support					
Fitness and Health					
Three or more times per week					
Arts					
Literacy					
Social-Competence					
Math Problem-Solving					
One or more times per week					
Science					
Technology					

Once a month	JAN	FEB	MAR	APR	MAY	JUN	JUL	AUG	SEP	OCT	NOV	DEC
Planning w/children and youth												
Community Service												
Three times per year (minimum)												
Family Event												

Section 3

Balancing the Schedule

Besides planning and evaluating the frequency with which program activities are offered, the following is a checklist that can help you ensure children's individual and developmental needs are addressed regularly.

Does Your Schedule Provide:

- An opportunity for children to relax and unwind?

- Time for children to adjust to the change in atmosphere and structure of the after-school setting?

- Group information sharing regarding the daily schedule or other important information?

- Time for children and youth to talk with staff on a one-on-one basis?

- Participation of children and youth in the preparation of snack?

- Time for children and youth to pursue special interests alone as well as in small groups?

- A balance of small/intimate versus large/collective gatherings and activities?

- Options for indoor and outdoor play?

- A balance of gross-motor activities versus relaxation and quiet time?

- The opportunity for children and youth to make choices?

- A balance of planned versus spontaneous activities initiated by children and staff?

- Smooth transitions through the use of consistency, preparation and options for individuals who finish activities early?

- A balance of competitive versus non-competitive activities and structures?

- Time for staff members to talk to one another and hold regular meetings?

- Time to plan, organize and review the progress of children and staff members?

- Time to communicate with parents at the end of the day and/or hold conferences?

- Breaks for staff?

- Time for clean up?

Evaluation

The final stage of curriculum planning concerns program evaluation. Parents, families, administrators, staff, employers, funders – even the children themselves – want to learn about the benefits, outcomes or results of participation in any program. Evaluation provides an important feedback loop to identify a program's strengths and weaknesses and determine its impact. Rather than thinking about evaluation after you have completed a program, you should think about how to evaluate your program's impact from the beginning. Thinking about it at the beginning will help guide decisions you make about activities and many other aspects of your program and will also make the process of evaluation easier because you will know from the start what sort of information you are looking for and need to collect.

Why Evaluate?

- To give program staff and participants a sense of purpose, intention and direction to all planning and activities.

- To collect information to determine progress, identify problems, reach goals.

- To establish credibility and accountability with funders, participants and staff by collecting data to balance against anecdotes or impressions.

- To provide opportunities for recognition and support when success is documented.

What to Assess?

There are two main types of evaluation: process and outcome.

1. *Process evaluation* is mainly concerned with the quality of what happened, i.e. how a program is being implemented. This may include who was served, what services were provided, the quality of the instruction associated with an activity, or the quality of the adult/child relationships. Before a determination is made about a program's impact, it is critical to know how well it was implemented.

2. *Outcome evaluation* focuses on the result or impact of the program, i.e. how well the program is achieving its goals. This may be measured through many means, including participant satisfaction or the change in children's abilities or knowledge.

It is critical for programs to determine what aspects of their program they want their evaluation to inform. Do they want basic facts about who the program is serving or do they want to know how well it is serving them? Do funders or administrators require a more extensive or specific evaluation? Determining the right evaluation questions can help program staff make sure the evaluation they conduct provides the answers they seek.

Determining the Right Evaluation Questions [15]	
In order to:	**Ask:**
Respond to participant needs	▪ How can we better serve our families? ▪ How do they view our program?
Respond to key stakeholders	▪ How do community members perceive our program? ▪ Why did our public relations efforts work?
Understand community resources and the need for additional services	▪ Is our community satisfied with our efforts?
Understand the services you provide and to whom you provide them	▪ Whom are we serving and how often? ▪ What are the most useful amounts and types of services?
Improve on what you are doing	▪ In what ways is our program tailored to unique family and youth circumstances? ▪ Are families and youth satisfied with the services we provide?
Describe and measure the impact of your services	▪ Are certain types and amounts of services more useful than others are for our youth and community?
Determine the costs of your program	▪ Is our program effective in attaining its stated goals? ▪ How much does our program cost, and are we providing services efficiently? ▪ Is there a way to market our successful strategies to ensure future financial support?

In addition to evaluating the overall program, it is important to evaluate specific activities. The following are potential questions to ask when evaluating activities:

- *Satisfaction* - Did the children enjoy the activity? (**NOTE:** You don't necessarily have to toss out activities that they didn't like. Sometimes the timing, ages, space or something else may have been "off" but the activity is still worth repeating.) Did the parents appreciate the value of the activity you provided?

- *Match of activities to goals or objectives* - Did the activity meet the program's goals or objectives? Over a month's time did the program introduce activities that met the program's objectives in all of the program's core content areas?

- *Match to standards* - Are activity choices high quality and consistent with national quality standards?

- *Making a difference* - Are activity choices making a difference in the lives of children and youth and/or their families? Are children and youth demonstrating new skills? Are they showing changes in their behavior?

[15] Adapted from: Little, Priscilla, Sharon DuPree, Sharon Deich. *Documenting Programs and Demonstrating Results: Evaluating Local Out-of-School Time Programs*, Harvard Family Research Project and The Finance Project. September 2002.

Assessing Environment

Upon entering a space of any kind, we make judgments. We tend to study what others are doing in this space to get a sense of what is allowed or expected. For example, soft chairs set close to each other says it's okay to socialize. Spaces for gathering and chatting often have a rug and small tables with food or snacks nearby. Spaces that invite exploration indicate that it's okay to make a small mess here, it's okay to spread your activity out here, and it's okay to try out your ideas here. Some spaces encourage children to be quiet; lighting is softer and seating is separate. In addition to an evaluation that focuses on programmatic choices, it is also important to assess a program's physical environment.

In high quality environments, staff link the space with the people who use it – through displays, pictures and artifacts that reflect the children, neighborhood, cultures and history of the place it is located in. Children's work is also displayed. These exhibits document and reveal children's interests and the ways the program attends to those interests.

The NAA Standards for Quality School-Age Care (see Section 4) include standards for both indoor and outdoor environments. These standards provide a baseline of quality and can be used to guide programs committed to providing children with unique growing and learning environments.

Linking Evaluation to Goals

In order to conduct an evaluation, you must have a clear understanding of your program's goals and objectives, as discussed earlier. Though it can be time consuming and difficult, setting clear objectives with measurable outcomes at the start will make the task of evaluation more manageable in the long run.

The Documentation Chart in Appendix B can help you keep track of the outcomes of specific activities in your program. This information will be useful to you or other staff who might offer this activity at another time. It can also aid in evaluation efforts by helping you to collect information as you proceed rather than having to go back and remember or re-create the outcomes of the activity long after it is finished.

Evaluation Resources

There are many levels of complexity in program evaluation. The type of evaluation your program is able to conduct will depend on many factors but especially resources, including time, administrative support and evaluation expertise. Below is a list of resources to learn more about evaluation and gain access to a wide array of evaluation tools.

1. **Beyond the Bell: A Toolkit for Creating Effective After-School Programs.** North Central Regional Educational Laboratory. Available for purchase on the Internet: **www.ncrel.org/after/bellkit.htm**

2. **Continuous Improvement Management Guide for 21ˢᵗ Century Community Learning Centers.** Available to download at: **www.ed.gov/offices/OUS/PES/21cent/cim226.pdf**

3. **Measuring and Evaluating Child Program Outcomes.** School-Age Review, 2000. Available for purchase from: **www.naa.org/publications.htm**

4. **The Out-of-School Time Learning and Development Project:** Harvard Family Research Project (HFRP) website (**www.hfrp.org**) provides access to many helpful tools and publications including:

    a. *Documenting Progress and Demonstrating Results: Evaluating Local Out-of-School Time Programs.* Written in collaboration with The Finance Project, this free booklet provides practitioners of local out-of-school time programs with an overview of evaluation basics as well as techniques, tools and strategies to track effectiveness over time.

    b. Out-of-School Time (OST) Program Evaluation Database provides accessible information about evaluation work of both large and small OST programs through a searchable database.

5. **The Program Manager's Guide to Evaluation,** Administration on Children, Youth and Families. Available to download from: **www.acf.dhhs.gov/programs/core/pubs_reports/prog_mgr.html**

6. **Use of Continuous Improvement and Evaluation in After-School Programs:** Final Report 2001. Prepared by the Center for Applied Research and Educational Improvement, College of Education and Human Development, University of Minnesota. **www.education.umn.edu/CAREI/Programs/mott/default.html**

Additional Curriculum Planning Resources

1. **Afterschool Alliance** is an alliance of public, private and non-profit groups committed to raising awareness and expanding resources for after-school programs. Initiated and currently coordinated by the C.S. Mott Foundation, the Alliance grew out of a partnership between the Foundation and the U.S. Department of Education. **www.afterschoolalliance.org**

2. **After-School.gov** is a clearinghouse of federal resources that support out-of-school time providers, programs and advocates. The site includes links to many of activities and abundant information on how to fund, start and operate an after-school program. **www.after-school.gov**

3. **Bringing Yourself to Work: Caregiving in After-School Environments** is a training model for after-school program staff that enables them to integrate self-knowledge and personal experience into their relationships with adults and children. **www.bringingyourselftowork.com**

4. **The Educational Resources Information Center (ERIC)** is a national information system designed to provide users with ready access to an extensive body of education-related literature. The ERIC database, the world's largest source of education information, contains nearly a million abstracts of documents and journal articles on education research and practice. **www.eric.ed.gov**

5. **Foundations, Inc.** operates extended-day enrichment programs and provides technical assistance to schools, school districts and other education and community organizations seeking to improve program performance and enhance student achievement in school and during non-school hours. **www.foundationsinc.org**

6. **Mid-Continental Regional Educational Laboratory (McREL)** is a U.S. Department of Education lab serving Colorado, Kansas, Missouri, Nebraska, North Dakota, South Dakota and Wyoming. McREL offers a searchable compendium of standards and benchmarks for K-12 education on their website. **www.mcrel.org**

7. **Museum Teaching Kits** bring the Children's Museum of Boston's hands-on, object-based learning philosophy straight to your program. Activities, supplies, videos, photos, models and artifacts from the museum's teaching collection foster cooperative, participatory learning and motivate a wide range of students. Available to rent by the week, the kits offer one- to four-week lesson plans in social studies, art, math, language arts, health and science. **www.bostonkids.org/kits/index.htm**

8. **National AfterSchool Association (formerly The National School-Age Care Alliance, NAA)** is a national membership organization supporting quality programs for school-age children and youth in their out-of-school hours. Established in 1987, NAA provides an umbrella organization to link people who work with school-age children and youth in a wide variety of agencies and settings. **www.naaweb.org**

9. **National Youth Development Information Center (NYDIC)** provides practice-related information about youth development to national and local youth-serving organizations at low or no cost. **www.nydic.org**

10. **Promising Practices in After-School (PPAS)** website provides a searchable database of promising practices from other after-school programs and a place to share your own good work with others to help build the field of after-school. **www.after-school.org/communicating.cfm**

11. **SAC-L Discussion List** is the place where administrators, caregivers/staff, policymakers, parents and others interested in school-age care can come together over the Internet to share ideas about school-age care planning, resources, activities, funding, staff and staff development and related subjects. SAC-L is co-owned by the National Institute on Out-of-School Time (NIOST) and by the Early Childhood and Parenting (ECAP) Collaborative at the University of Illinois. **http://ecap.crc.uiuc.edu/listserv/sac-l.html**

12. **School-Age Notes** is a resource organization that develops and provides information, technical assistance and resources concerning children and youth in out-of-school settings before-and-after-school and during vacations. **www.AfterSchoolCatalog.com**

Discussion Questions for Section Three

1. Describe the mission, goals and objectives of your after-school program. (If you don't run or work in an after-school program, describe an imaginary mission of a program that you would like to work for.)

2. Describe the activities that occur in your program (or imagined program) which address the mission and objectives of the program. Describe how the activities and objectives relate to and support each other. How are they similar or different from the program activities described in the daily schedule on page 38?

3. Using the six concepts for choosing activities described in this section, think about your program (or imagined program) and describe how these criteria are reflected in the program's choice of activities.

   - What are the needs and interests of the children?
   - What are the goals and objectives of your program?
   - How do children learn and develop?
   - What are the limits and assets of the program's space and resources?
   - What is your teaching style and what are your strengths?
   - What is the daily schedule at your program?

4. Refer to any collection or booklet of activities (including this guide) and choose 3 to 5 activities you would like to try in your program. Share your choices with others and explain the reasons you made these particular choices.

5. Using these choices, create a schedule showing when you would introduce them during the week, and how you would get kids interested in doing them.

NOTES

Section Four:

Linking Activities to Benchmarks and Standards

Learning Benchmarks

Linking Activities to Learning Standards

Linking Activities to Quality Standards

Sample Learning Benchmarks

- Language Arts Standards
- Mathematics Standards
- Science Standards
- Arts Education Standards
- Social-Competence Benchmarks
- Fitness and Nutrition Benchmarks
- Technology Benchmarks

Sample Quality Standards

- National AfterSchool Association Standards (NAA)
- School-Age Care Environment Rating Scale (SACERS)
- Search Institute's 40 Developmental Assets

Section 4

NOTES

Links to Learning: *A Curriculum Planning Guide for After-School Programs*

Section Four

Linking Activities to Benchmarks and Standards

When planning curriculum or selecting activities it is critical to link the activities to learning benchmarks and quality standards. "Learning benchmarks" are guidelines created by educators or other experts to provide guidance to teachers, parents and others to know what children and youth should be expected to know or learn at different ages or stages of development. Linking after-school activities to learning benchmarks helps providers deliberately examine the ways the program is supporting children's learning. "Quality" standards are equally important in providing valid measures and guidelines to help you ascertain and continuously improve the quality of your program.

Learning Benchmarks

Almost every activity in an after-school program has a natural link to more than one academic subject area, i.e. reading, math, science, etc. For example: [16]

Activity	Literacy	Math	Science	Arts
Cooking activity (ages 6-8)	• Reading the recipe • Writing a shopping list	• Measuring the ingredients	• Practice reasoning and hypothesizing • Observing effects of moisture and heat	• Food presentation color, shape, texture, decoration
Theater group (ages 9-11)	• Reading or writing a script • Writing a program or poster	• Measuring to build a set • Budgeting for costumes • Selling tickets	• (Not applicable)	• Learning to sing, act, play an instrument, etc. • Creating costumes or posters
Walking club (ages 11-14)	• Writing reflective or poetic accounts • Reading or listening to nature stories, essays or poems	• Calculating distances traveled • Measuring rainfall or plant growth	• Observing the natural world • Researching the observed wildlife or plants	• Sketching or photographing wildlife or landscapes • Collecting items during the walk to make collages

_____

[16] Template adapted from Hampshire Educational Collaborative. Activity Planning template developed by Susan O'Connor.

Section 4

State Departments of Education define the benchmarks or standards that teachers use to choose the school day activities. Program staff can check with their local Department of Education for a copy of the city, town or state's learning standards and examine how their activities align with the standards and create closer links between school and after-school. Many times these standards can also be found online at the relevant agency's website. [17]

In addition to reviewing standards developed locally, programs can look to general standards developed by national organizations with content expertise (e.g. The American Association for the Advancement of Science) to complement the learning that is happening in school. At the end of this section, you will find examples of national benchmarks for literacy, math, science, arts, social competence, fitness and nutrition and technology that can help you align your activities with general learning benchmarks.

Linking Activities to Learning Standards

The best way to establish a link between an activity and a learning standard is to:

- Plan for the activity and think about the potential learning opportunities and the academic content areas it may relate to.

- Obtain the learning standards your town, city or state has established for the primary or core curriculum areas (math, science, language, history, arts, etc.).

- Look through the standards associated with the appropriate content areas for the age level of the children who will do the activity to find the standards that relate most closely to the activity. If you can't make a match of an activity to a listed learning standard, it may still be a valuable experience for the children doing the activity and you should check it against your program's mission/goals.

- After doing the activity, go back to look at the standards that you thought it would match and see if you were correct and if there were other learning opportunities that you didn't anticipate. Having actually done the activity with children you will have a much better sense of what was learned and the curriculum area(s) with which the activity was most closely associated.

Linking Activities to Quality Standards

As the after-school field has grown and developed, there have been increasing efforts to define and articulate effectiveness and quality. The following list are characteristics of after-school programs that have been determined to be necessary to support both children's academic success and their overall development.

---

[17] Midcontinent Research for Education and Learning (McREL) offers a searchable compendium of standards and benchmarks for K-12 education on their website. This is a great site for becoming familiar with the content standards established by different states. http://www.mcrel.org/standards%2Dbenchmarks/

Key Elements of Effective After-School Programs [18]

- Safe, stable places

- Basic care and services

- Caring relationships

- Relevant, challenging experiences

- Networks and connections

- High expectations and standards

- Opportunities for voice, choice and contribution

- Personalized, high-quality instruction

In addition to linking to learning standards, programs should always be examining the activities they offer through the lens of quality – does this activity meet the highest quality standards? There are an increasing number of tools that can help program staff determine program quality. Among the best currently available tools are the National AfterSchool Association's NAA Standards for Quality School-Age Care and School-Age Care Environment Rating Scale (SACERS) standards. [19]

The following sample demonstrates a tool staff can use to deliberately examine how activities relate both to learning and quality standards.

---

[18] Pittman, K., Irby, M., Tolman, J., Yohalem, N., & Ferber, T, "Preventing problems, promoting development, encouraging engagement: Competing priorities or inseparable goals." Forum for Youth Investment. Washington, DC. 2001.

[19] See the end of this section for summaries of both NAA and SACERS standards.

Linking Activities to Learning Benchmarks and Quality Standards [20]

Activity Title	The Panther, The Chicken and the Bag of Grain Problem						
Description	Tell children story of man trying to get a panther, chicken and grain over to his island in a rowboat, one at a time, etc. Task: Figure out which purchase to take first, second and third, so that all of them will survive, long enough to get them to the island in his boat which will carry only him and one of the things he purchased at a time.*						

Core Content Area (check all that apply)	Math	Literacy	Science	Arts	Fitness/ Nutrition	Social Competence	Other
	✓						

Skills for the New Economy (check all that apply)	Numeracy	Communication		Problem solving	Technology	Work w/ others
		✓		✓		

Quality Standards	**NAA** #13 – Children have a chance to join enrichment activities that promote basic skills and higher level thinking	**SACERS** 25. Math/reasoning activities	**OTHER** Search Institute's 40 Developmental Assets #22 – young person actively engaged in learning

	Standard	**Grade/Age**	**Description**
Benchmark or Learning Standard	National Council of Teachers of Mathematics: #1 – Mathematics as Problem Solving	K-4 5-8	▪ Use problem solving to investigate and understand math concepts ▪ Problems from everyday mathematical situations ▪ Variety of strategies and emphasis on multi-step and non-routine problems

*Answer: Take the chicken in the boat first, panthers don't eat grain. Drop the chicken off at the island. Row back. Take the panther in the boat next, leaving the bag of grain till last. Once you get to the island, drop the panther off, but pick up the chicken again. Put the chicken back in the boat and row back to the mainland. Pick up the bag of grain. Drop the chicken off at the mainland. Take the grain to the island and drop it off, leaving the chicken behind. Row back alone to pick up the chicken again, and bring it back to the island.

---

[20] Template adapted from Hampshire Educational Collaborative. Activity Planning template developed by Susan O'Connor.

Sample Learning Benchmarks
Language Arts (4th Ed.) Standards

Writing
- Uses the general skills and strategies of the writing process
- Uses the stylistic and rhetorical aspects of writing
- Uses grammatical and mechanical conventions in written compositions
- Gathers and uses information for research purposes

Reading
- Uses the general skills and strategies of the reading process
- Uses reading skills and strategies to understand and interpret a variety of literary texts
- Uses reading skills and strategies to understand and interpret a variety of informational texts

Listening and Speaking
- Uses listening and speaking strategies for different purposes

Viewing
- Uses viewing skills and strategies to understand and interpret visual media

Media
- Understands the characteristics and components of the media

Topics
- Applying technology
- Conversation and group discussion
- Creating support
- Critical listening
- Critical reading
- Critical viewing
- Critically evaluating written/spoken texts and visual media
- Decoding/Word identification
- Grammar and usage
- Informational genres
- Informative writing
- Language in daily use
- Literary genres
- Literary style and techniques
- Literacy/Narrative writing
- Locating sources/gathering information
- Mass media format
- Media and society
- Media production
- Oral composition and presentation
- Organizing information and ideas
- Paragraph development

- Personal response to written/spoken texts and visual media
- Persuasive writing
- Phonological awareness
- Reading and comprehension strategies
- Reading fundamentals
- Story/Literary elements
- Styles and techniques in visual media
- Style, diction and voice
- Verbal and nonverbal communication
- Visual media genres
- Writing conventions/mechanics
- Writing for audience and purpose
- Writing format
- Writing fundamentals
- Writing process
- Writing research papers

Mathematics (4th Ed.) Standards

- Uses a variety of strategies in the problem-solving process
- Understands and applies basic and advanced properties of the concepts of numbers
- Uses basic and advanced procedures while performing the processes of computation
- Understands and applies basic and advanced properties of the concepts of measurement
- Understands and applies basic and advanced properties of the concepts of geometry
- Understands and applies basic and advanced concepts of statistics and data analysis
- Understands and applies basic and advanced concepts of probability
- Understands and applies basic and advanced properties of functions and algebra
- Understands the general nature and uses of mathematics

Topics
- Addition/subtraction
- Analytic geometry
- Basic and linear measures
- Communicating about mathematics
- Data collection and sampling
- Data distribution
- Data organization and display
- Decimals

- Equations and inequalities
- Estimation
- Experimental probability
- Exponents/logarithms/roots
- Expressions
- Factors/multiples/primes
- Formulating/testing hypotheses
- Fractions
- Functions
- Graphs and graphing systems
- Integers
- Likelihood/chance/certainty
- Lines and angles
- Mathematical enterprise
- Mathematical reasoning
- Mathematics, science and technology
- Matrices
- Measurement estimation
- Motion Geometry/transformations
- Multiplication/division
- Number systems
- Patterns
- Perimeter/area/circumference
- Perimeter/area/volume
- Permutations/combinations
- Precision/accuracy
- Problem-solving
- Proof and empirical verification
- Rate
- Ratio/proportion/percent
- Reasoning and predicting for data
- Representing problems
- Sequences and series
- Sets
- Shapes and figures
- Similarity and congruence
- Solution strategies
- Triangles
- Trigonometry
- Units of measurement
- Uses of mathematics
- Variables
- Vectors

Section 4

- Volume/capacity
- Weight and mass
- Whole numbers/place value/numeration

Science (4th Ed.) Standards

Earth and Space Sciences
- Understands atmospheric processes and the water cycle
- Understands Earth's composition and structure
- Understands the composition and structure of the universe and the Earth's place in it

Life Sciences
- Understands the principles of heredity and related concepts
- Understands the structure and function of cells and organisms
- Understands relationships among organisms and their physical environment
- Understands biological evolution and the diversity of life

Physical Sciences
- Understands the structure and properties of matter
- Understands the sources and properties of energy
- Understands forces and motion

Nature of Science
- Understands the nature of scientific knowledge
- Understands the nature of scientific inquiry
- Understands the scientific enterprise

Topics
- Ability to support life
- Atomic structure
- Atoms and molecules
- Biogeochemical cycles
- Characteristics of organisms
- Characteristics of the Earth system
- Chemical reaction
- Classification of organisms
- Conservation of matter and energy
- Diversity and unity among organisms
- Earth's atmosphere
- Earth's history
- Earth's surface features
- Electricity and magnetism
- Energy in the Earth system
- Energy transfer and entropy
- Ethics in science
- Forces and motion

- Forms of energy
- Genetic mutation and recombination
- Gravity
- Interdependence of organisms
- Life cycles
- Matter and energy in living systems
- Molecular basis of heredity
- Motion of the Earth and Moon
- Natural selection and biological evolution
- Nuclear reactions and forces
- People in science
- Plate tectonics
- Populations and ecosystems
- Positions and motion
- Properties of substances
- Regulation and behavior
- Relationships between organisms and the environment
- Reproduction
- Rock cycle
- Rocks, minerals and soil
- Science, technology and society
- Scientific collaboration and communication
- Scientific data collection/analysis/interpretation
- Scientific explanations
- Scientific investigation
- Scientific investigation/repeatability
- Scientific knowledge
- Seasons, weather and climate
- States of matter
- Structure and function in cells
- Structure and function in organisms
- Survival and extinction
- The Solar System
- The Sun and other stars
- The Universe
- Vibrations and waves
- Water in the Earth system

Arts Education Standards
Dance (K-4)

- Identifies and demonstrates movement elements and skills in performing dance
- Understands choreographic principles, processes and structures

- Understands dance as a way to create a community meaning
- Applies and demonstrates critical and creative thinking skills in dance
- Demonstrates and understands dance in various cultures and historical periods
- Making connection between dance and healthful living
- Making connections between dance and other disciplines

Music (K-4)

- Sings alone and with others, a varied repertoire of music
- Performs on instruments, alone and with others, a varied repertoire of music
- Improvises melodies, variations, and accompaniments
- Composes and arranges music within specified guidelines
- Reads and notates music
- Listens to, analyzes, and describes music
- Evaluates music and music performances
- Understands relationships between music, the other arts, and disciplines outside the arts
- Understands music in relation to history and culture

Theater (K-4)

- Writes scripts by planning and recording improvisations based on personal experience and heritage, imagination, literature, and history
- Engages in acting by assuming roles and interacting in improvisations
- Designs by visualizing and arranging environments for classroom dramatizations
- Directs by planning classroom dramatizations
- Researches by finding information to support classroom dramatizations
- Compares and connects art forms by describing theater, dramatic media (such as film, television, and electronic media), and other art forms
- Analyzes and explains personal preferences and constructs meanings from classroom dramatizations and from theater, film, television, and electronic media productions
- Understands context by recognizing the role of theater, film, television, and electronic media in daily life

Visual Arts (K-4)

- Understands and applies media, techniques, and processes
- Uses knowledge of structures and functions
- Chooses and evaluates a range of subject matter, symbols, and ideas
- Understands the visual arts in relation to history and cultures
- Reflects upon and assesses the characteristics and merits of their work and the work of others
- Makes connections between visual arts and other disciplines

Dance (5-8)

- Identifies and demonstrates movement elements and skills in performing dance
- Understands choreographic principles, processes, and structures

- Understands dance as a way to create and communicate meaning
- Applies and demonstrates critical and creative thinking skills in dance
- Demonstrates and understands dance in various cultures and historical periods
- Makes connections between dance and healthful living
- Makes connections between dance and other disciplines

Music (5-8)

- Sings, alone and with others, a varied repertoire of music
- Performs on instruments, alone and with others, a varied repertoire of music
- Improvises melodies, variations, and accompaniments
- Composes and arranges music within specified guidelines
- Reads and notates music
- Listens to, analyzes, and describes music
- Evaluates music and music performances
- Understands relationships between music, the other arts, and disciplines outside the arts
- Understands music in relation to history and culture

Theater (5-8)

- Writes scripts by the creation of improvisations and scripted scenes based on personal experience and heritage, imagination, literature, and history
- Acts by developing basic acting skills to portray characters who interact in improvised and scripted scenes
- Designs by developing environments for improvised and scripted scenes
- Directs by organizing rehearsals for improvised and scripted scenes
- Researches by using cultural and historical information to support improvised and scripted scenes
- Compares and incorporates art forms by analyzing methods of presentation and audience response for theater, dramatic media (such as film, television, and electronic media), and other art forms
- Analyzes, evaluates, and constructs meanings from improvised and scripted scenes and from theater, film, television, and electronic media productions
- Understands context by analyzing the role of theater, film, television, and electronic media in the community and in other cultures

Visual Arts (5-8)

- Understands and applies media, techniques, and processes
- Uses knowledge of structures and functions
- Chooses and evaluates a range of subject matter, symbols, and ideas
- Understands the visual arts in relation to history and cultures
- Reflects upon and assesses the characteristics and merits of their work and the work of others
- Makes connections between visual arts and other disciplines

Social-Competence Benchmarks

The Collaborative for Academic, Social, and Emotional Learning (CASEL) has identified the following five social competence skill clusters[21] as essential for maintaining relationships with others. These standards can be useful to after-school programs seeking concrete terms to describe the social competence skills they seek to teach in their programs.

Self-Awareness

- **Identifying emotions:** Identifying and labeling one's feelings

- **Recognizing strengths:** Identifying and cultivating one's strengths and positive qualities

Social Awareness

- **Perspective-taking:** Identifying and understanding the thoughts and feelings of others

- **Appreciating diversity:** Understanding that individual and group differences complement each other and make the world more interesting

Self-Management

- **Managing emotions:** Monitoring and regulating feelings so they aid rather than impede the handling of situations

- **Goal setting:** Establishing and working toward the achievement of short- and long-term pro-social goals

Responsible Decision Making

- **Analyzing situations:** Accurately perceiving situations in which a decision is to be made and assessing factors that might influence one's response

- **Assuming personal responsibility:** Recognizing and understanding one's obligation to engage in ethical, safe and legal behaviors

- **Respecting others:** Believing that others deserve to be treated with kindness and compassion and feeling motivated to contribute to the common good

- **Problem solving:** Generating, implementing, and evaluating positive and informed solutions to problems

Relationship Skills

- **Communication:** Using verbal and nonverbal skills to express oneself and promote positive and effective exchanges with others

- **Building relationships:** Establishing and maintaining healthy and rewarding connections with individuals and groups

- **Negotiation:** Achieving mutually satisfactory resolutions to conflict by addressing the needs of all concerned

- **Refusal:** Effectively conveying and following through with one's decision not to engage in unwanted, unsafe, unethical, or unlawful conduct

---

[21] CASEL Social Emotional Learning Competencies. Copyright 2000-2003.
www.casel.org/about_sel/SELskills.php

NATIONAL CONTENT STANDARDS for PHYSICAL EDUCATION [22]
Grades K - 12

A Physically Educated Student:

- Demonstrates competency in many movement forms and proficiency in a few movement forms.
- Applies movement concepts and principles to the learning and development of motor skills.
- Exhibits a physically active lifestyle.
- Achieves and maintains a health-enhancing level of physical fitness.
- Demonstrates responsible personal and social behavior in physical activity settings.
- Demonstrates understanding and respect for differences among people in physical activity settings.
- Understands that physical activity provides opportunities for enjoyment, challenge, self-expression, and social interaction.

NUTRITION BENCHMARKS [23]

Nutrition activities and programs help children and youth:

- Gain a better understanding of the USDA Food Guide Pyramid and how to use it to make healthy food choices each day (including healthy choices when eating fast food).

- Gain a better understanding of basic nutritional requirements, food labels and the nutritional contents of items in their daily diets.

- Understand food safety issues and behaviors.

Section 4

---

[22] The National Association for Sport and Physical Education, in association with the American Alliance for Health, Physical Education, Recreation and Dance, 2003. www.aahperd.org/naspe

[23] These nutrition learning benchmarks are a composite created from examining many different nutrition programs, learning objectives and activities, and they apply to all ages.

Technology Benchmarks
Technology Foundation Standards for All Students [24]

Basic operations and concepts
- Students demonstrate a sound understanding of the nature and operation of technology systems.
- Students are proficient in the use of technology.

Social, ethical, and human issues
- Students understand the ethical, cultural, and societal issues related to technology.
- Students practice responsible use of technology systems, information, and software.
- Students develop positive attitudes toward technology uses that support lifelong learning, collaboration, personal pursuits, and productivity.

Technology productivity tools
- Students use technology tools to enhance learning, increase productivity, and promote creativity.
- Students use productivity tools to collaborate in constructing technology-enhanced models, prepare publications, and produce other creative works.

Technology communications tools
- Students use telecommunications to collaborate, publish, and interact with peers, experts and other audiences.
- Students use a variety of media and formats to communicate information and ideas effectively to multiple audiences.

Technology research tools
- Students use technology to locate, evaluate, and collect information from a variety of sources.
- Students use technology tools to process data and report results.
- Students evaluate and select new information resources and technological innovations based on the appropriateness for specific tasks.

Technology problem-solving and decision-making tools
- Students use technology resources for solving problems and making informed decisions.
- Students employ technology in the development of strategies for solving problems in the real world.

---

[24] These standards were developed by the International Society for Technology in Education National Educational Technology Standards for Students (ISTENETS), © 2000-2004, and can be found at: http://cnets.iste.org/students/s_stands.html. The NETS Project has also developed "Profiles for Technology Literate Students," which describe specific technology competence students should exhibit from PreK-12. These can be found at: http://cnets.iste.org/students/s_profiles.html

Sample Quality Standards

The National AfterSchool Association (NAA) Standards for Quality School-Age Care [25]

The following list summarizes the 36 observable NAA quality standards listed under six categories.

Human Relationships

1. Staff relate to all children and youth in positive ways.
2. Staff respond appropriately to the individual needs of children and youth.
3. Staff encourage children and youth to make choices and to become more responsible.
4. Staff interact with children and youth to help them learn.
5. Staff use positive techniques to guide the behavior of children and youth.
6. Children and youth generally interact with each other in positive ways.
7. Staff and families interact with each other in positive ways.
8. Staff work well together to meet the needs of children and youth.

Indoor Environment

9. The program's indoor space meets the needs of children and youth.
10. The indoor space allows children and youth to take initiative and explore their interests.

Outdoor Environment

11. The outdoor play area meets the needs of children and youth, and the equipment allows them to be independent and creative.

Activities

12. The daily schedule is flexible, and it offers enough security, independence and stimulation to meet the needs of all children and youth.
13. Children and youth can choose from a wide variety of activities.
14. Activities reflect the mission of the program and promote the development of all the children and youth in the program.
15. There are sufficient materials to support program activities.

Safety, Health, and Nutrition

16. The safety and security of children and youth are protected.
17. The program provides an environment that protects and enhances the health of children and youth.
18. The program staff work to protect and enhance the health of children and youth.
19. Children and youth are carefully supervised to maintain safety.
20. The program serves food and drinks that meet the needs of children and youth.

---

[25] More detailed information about each standard above can be found in: *The NAA Standards For Quality School-Age Care* booklet available from the National AfterSchool Association. www.naaweb.org

Administration

21. Staff/child ratios and group sizes permit the staff to meet the needs of children and youth.
22. Children and youth are supervised at all times.
23. Staff support families' involvement in the program.
24. Staff, families and schools share important information to support the well-being of children and youth.
25. The program builds links to the community.
26. The program's indoor space meets the needs of staff.
27. The outdoor space is large enough to meet the needs of children, youth and staff.
28. Staff, children and youth work together to plan and implement suitable activities, which are consistent with the program's philosophy.
29. Program policies and procedures are in place to protect the safety of the children and youth.
30. Program policies exist to protect and enhance the health of all children and youth.
31. All staff are professionally qualified to work with children and youth.
32. Staff (paid, volunteer and substitute) are given an orientation to the job before working with children and youth.
33. The training needs of the staff are assessed, and training is relevant to the responsibilities of each job. Assistant Group Leaders receive at least 15 hours of training annually. Group Leaders receive at least 18 hours of training annually. Senior Group Leaders receive at least 21 hours of training annually. Program Administrators receive at least 30 hours of training annually.
34. Staff receive appropriate support to make their work experience positive.
35. The administration provides sound management of the program.
36. Program policies and procedures are responsive to the needs of children, youth and families in the community.

School-Age Care Environment Rating Scale (SACERS) [26]

The following list provides an overview of the 49 items and 7 subscales of the SACERS:

Space and Furnishings

1. Indoor space
2. Space for gross motor activities
3. Space for privacy
4. Room arrangement
5. Furnishings for routine care
6. Furnishings for learning and recreational activities
7. Furnishings for relaxation and comfort
8. Furnishings for gross motor activities
9. Access to host facilities
10. Space to meet personal needs of staff
11. Space to meet professional needs of staff

Health and Safety

12. Health policy
13. Health practices
14. Emergency and safety policy
15. Safety practice
16. Attendance
17. Departure
18. Meals/snacks
19. Personal hygiene

Activities

20. Arts and crafts
21. Music and movement
22. Blocks and construction
23. Drama/theater
24. Language/reading activities
25. Math/reasoning activities
26. Science/nature activities
27. Cultural awareness

Interactions

28. Greeting/departing
29. Staff-child interactions
30. Staff-child communication
31. Staff supervision of children
32. Discipline
33. Peer interactions
34. Interactions between staff and parents
35. Staff interaction
36. Relationship between program staff and classroom teachers

Program Structure

37. Schedule
38. Free choice
39. Relationship between program staff and program host
40. Use of community resources

Staff Development

41. Opportunities for professional growth
42. Staff meetings
43. Supervision and evaluation of staff

Special Needs Supplementary Items

44. Provisions for exceptional children
45. Individualization
46. Multiple opportunities for learning and practicing skills
47. Engagement
48. Peer interactions
49. Promoting communication

Section 4

---

[26] More detailed information about the School-Age Care Environment Rating Scale (SACERS) can be found at the website of the Frank Porter Graham Child Development Institute. www.fpg.unc.edu/~ecers/sacersoverview_frame.html

Search Institute's 40 Developmental Assets [27]

The Search Institute has identified a framework of 40 developmental assets – building blocks of healthy development – that help adolescents grow up healthy, caring and responsible. They have similar asset lists for other age groups including toddlers, preschoolers and elementary-age children. Though not quality standards per se, programs can use this list to determine if they are helping children and youth develop the personal and social assets they need to succeed.

External Assets

Support:

1. **Family Support:** Family life provides high levels of love and support.
2. **Positive Family Communication**: Young person and her or his parent(s) communicate positively and young person is willing to seek advice and counsel from parents.
3. **Other Adult Relationships:** Young person receives support from three or more nonparent adults.
4. **Caring Neighborhood:** Young person experiences caring neighbors.
5. **Caring School Climate:** School provides a caring, encouraging environment.
6. **Parent Involvement in Schooling:** Parents are actively involved in helping young person succeed in school.

Empowerment:

7. **Community Values Youth:** Young person perceives that adults in the community value youth.
8. **Youth as Resources:** Young people are given useful roles in the community.
9. **Service to Others:** Young person serves in the community one hour or more per week.
10. **Safety:** Young person feels safe at home, school and in the neighborhood.

Boundaries and Expectations:

11. **Family Boundaries:** Family has clear rules and consequences and monitors the young person's whereabouts.
12. **School Boundaries:** School provides clear rules and consequences.
13. **Neighborhood Boundaries:** Neighbors take responsibility for monitoring young people's behavior.
14. **Adult Role Models:** Parent(s) and other adults model positive, responsible behavior.
15. **Positive Peer Influence:** Young person's best friends model responsible behavior.
16. **High Expectations:** Both parent(s) and teachers encourage the young person to do well.

---

[27] 40 Developmental Assets, Search Institute, www.search-institute.org

Constructive Use of Time:

17. **Creative Activities:** Young person spends three or more hours per week in lessons or practice in music, theater or other arts.

18. **Youth Programs:** Young person spends three or more hours per week in sports, clubs or organizations at school and/or in the community.

19. **Youth Programs:** Young person spends one or more hours per week in activities in a religious institution.

20. **Time at Home:** Young person is out with friends "with nothing special to do" two or fewer nights per week.

Internal Assets

Commitment to Learning:

21. **Achievement/Motivation:** Young person is motivated to do well in school.

22. **School Engagement:** Young person is actively engaged in learning.

23. **Homework:** Young person reports doing at least one hour of homework every school day.

24. **Bonding to School:** Young person cares about her or his school.

25. **Reading for Pleasure:** Young person reads for pleasure three or more hours per week.

Positive Values:

26. **Caring:** Young person places high value on helping other people.

27. **Equality and Social Justice:** Young person places high value on promoting equality and reducing hunger and poverty.

28. **Integrity:** Young person acts on convictions and stands up for her or his beliefs.

29. **Honesty:** Young person "tells the truth even when it is not easy."

30. **Responsibility:** Young person accepts and takes personal responsibility.

31. **Restraint:** Young person believes it is important not to be sexually active or to use alcohol or other drugs.

Social-Competencies:

32. **Planning and Decision-Making:** Young person knows how to plan ahead and make choices.

33. **Interpersonal Competence:** Young person has empathy, sensitivity, and friendship skills.

34. **Cultural Competence:** Young person has knowledge of and comfort with people of different cultural/racial/ethnic backgrounds.

35. **Resistance Skills:** Young person can resist negative peer pressure and dangerous situations.

36. **Peaceful Conflict Resolution:** Young person seeks to resolve conflict nonviolently.

Section 4

Positive Identity:

37. **Personal Power:** Young person feels he or she has control over "things that happen to me."

38. **Self-Esteem:** Young person reports having a high self-esteem.

39. **Sense of Purpose:** Young person reports that "my life has a purpose."

40. **Positive View of Personal Future:** Young person is optimistic about her or his personal future.

Discussion Questions for Section Four

1. Refer to the "Activities" section of the NAA standards on page 68. Use these to assess activities at your site, a site you visit or an after-school program you can observe in a video. Of the standards, which were poorly met? What ideas do you have for improving them?

2. Refer to the Learning Benchmarks in the core content areas in this chapter and determine which benchmarks were addressed by the activities you observed.

3. Think about the qualities of the spaces and environments in which you are most comfortable or happy. Which of these qualities are found in your after-school program? Which are not but might be possible to include? How might you go about including them?

Section Five:

Theme- and Project-Based Learning

Theme-Based Activities

- Good Theme Characteristics
- Developing Theme-Based Activities

Project-Based Learning

- Why Project-Based Learning Activities in After-School?
- Good Project Characteristics
- Project-Based Learning Activity Requirements
- Project Phases
- Sample Project-Based Activities
- Additional Project-Based Learning Resources

Section 5

NOTES

Links to Learning: *A Curriculum Planning Guide for After-School Programs*

Section Five
Theme- and Project-Based Learning

Theme-Based Activities

A theme is an all-encompassing title for a wide range of activities that relate to a specific topic. A theme such as "Animal Habitats" is a way to organize activities that have to do with studying animals and where they live. Since activities within a theme can cover many different learning areas (math, science, literacy, arts), themes tend to include multiple kinds of learning experiences and ensure that every child will participate in something of interest. Planning an activity menu around a theme also gives a staff person a creative frame of reference.

In choosing a theme, keeping it broad maximizes the range of activities. For example, "Horseshoe Magnets" is very specific. "Magnets," on the other hand, is broader and allows for a variety of activities using a variety of magnets. "Making Magnets Work for Us" is an even better theme title. It implies that exploration, experimentation, invention and application could occur within the chosen activities. Some themes can be expanded into long-term projects or be made into permanent program or club titles.

Good Theme Characteristics
Activities associated with any theme should:

- Be pre-planned by staff, children and youth (and perhaps parents).

- Include physical activity: children and youth want to move and do things.

- Encourage children to understand how concepts are connected to each other, apply their emerging skills to new activities, and master or practice acquired skills.

- Allow children to show competence and achievement.

- Provide opportunities for children and youth to learn about themselves.

- Help children and youth find out things about the world they never knew and spark new interests.

- Invite, respect, and support creative expression.

- Encourage positive social interaction (collaboration, cooperation, and "giving back").

- Support academic skill development and understanding specific concepts.

Sample themes include:

- ***Neighborhood Animals*** – all about the animals that live in the neighborhood.

- ***Inventions*** – a design and testing experience.

- ***Schoolyard Ecology*** – a weather, animal and plant study.

- ***The Arts in Our Community*** – an opportunity to find out more about arts.

- ***Who Lives in Our Community?*** – an in-depth look at the people in the community.

Developing Theme-Based Activities

Step 1: *Brainstorm and Develop an Activity Web*

An activity web reveals all the possible concepts and activities related to a theme that children and adults come up with during a brainstorming session. The activity web example shown here begins with the words "Out-of-Doors: The Park" in the center of a huge sheet of paper. It illustrates a great number of ideas generated during a brainstorming session, where children and youth shared any activity ideas that came into their heads. Only some of the activities may be feasible because of limitations imposed by program environment and space, schedules, materials, budget, staff knowledge and the ages of the children.

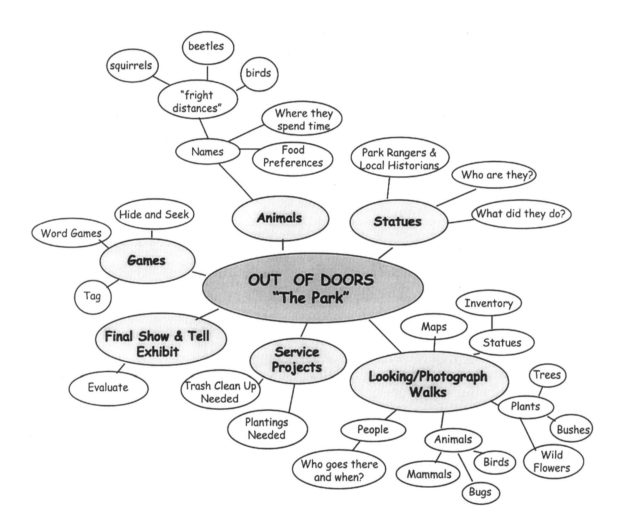

Links to Learning: *A Curriculum Planning Guide for After-School Programs*

Tips for Brainstorming an Activity Web

- **Introduction:** "Let's get out-of-doors. It's been a while since we've done that. Where's an outdoor place you'd like to spend some time getting to know better?"

- **Discuss a theme title:** "The Park" is the suggestion the children seem to prefer. Write the words "Out of Doors: The Park" in the center of a huge sheet of paper and draw a circle around it.

- **Brainstorm:** Ask "What do you think we might see in the park?" The children brainstorm what they know about the park and share guesses about what they think they might see at the park. Refer to suggestions with more questions, "What could we do or find out about the animals that live in the park?"

- **Record:** Each guess (animals, statues, plants, people, water, etc.) is written on the sheet of paper surrounding the center theme title circle ("The Park"). From these guesses, the children can suggest related activities associated with each. Draw a circle around each item and draw a thin line to connect it to the theme title.

- **Organizing the web:** As the children share their activity ideas, write down each idea near the topic associated with it, circle it, and draw a line to connect it to its topic. Circling words is important because it keeps ideas separated but connected to their source. By the time you have finished brainstorming, there will be a lot of information scattered on the page. Circling ideas helps create order and make sense of it all.

- **Connect to objectives:** Enter the program's goals and objectives into the web design in order to continue the process of suggesting and brainstorming examples of activities.

- **Keep developing:** Some activity ideas may branch into even more specific activities. For example, in the Out of Doors web example (see web diagram), the "Fright Distance" activity (i.e. how close can you get to an animal before it is frightened away); the "Food Preferences?" activity; and the "Where do animals spend most of their time?" activities all originated in the Animals section. Some of these activities could branch even further. For example, "Fright Distances" can be expanded to include activities regarding how close you can approach birds, squirrels and insects.

Step 2: *Determine Children's Preferences*

Once the web has been designed, find out about the children's activity preferences. Asking the children to vote for their favorite activities (the ones the program can support) is a sure-fire way to create a wonderful collection of related activities that children have already "bought into."

Invite interested children to form a Leadership Club to meet with you to tally and discuss the selected activities. These leaders will help gather materials, take responsibility for a smaller group of children and assist in implementing activities. Leadership Club members can also develop an action plan for each activity and evaluate each one in order to improve it.

Section 5

Step 3: *Develop an Activity Plan*

See the Developing an Activity Plan tips in Section 3 and work through the steps with the children.

Step 4: *Day Two and Beyond*

If the children vote to begin with Animals, the first activities may include identifying, photographing, naming and counting all the animals that can be found in the park. This activity may take several days and may involve assigning groups of children to look for and photograph one particular kind of animal.

Extensions:

- Choose other activities from the web that match the weather realities, the mood of the children, and your budget for the theme study. Because picture taking, displaying, counting and identifying can become tedious if done too much or too often, you might suggest the children bring balls, ropes and chalk for playing games suitable for a park. Or have local historians, storytellers and park rangers meet with the children to tell them about the people depicted in the various statues.

Step 5: *Conclude the Study*

Conclude the study while enthusiasm for the activities is still high among the children and staff. Every theme study should finish with an activity that somehow wraps up the children's experiences. The concluding event can include a final "show and tell" of the photographs they took, a presentation to the general public that winds up in the newspaper or an official recognition of the community service by town officials or the people most helped by the project.

Step 6: *Evaluation*

Often the best evaluation is the children's opinions about the activities. Provide children with a list of all the activities and ask them to rate them on a scale. (See Appendix B for a simple satisfaction survey.)

Outcomes are easier to determine when you know what you wanted the children and youth to gain (skills, knowledge or behavior changes) from participating in the thematic activities. These objectives and expected outcomes will be part of your planning process (see Section 3). For after-school programs, the social skills of collaboration, helping each other, displaying respect, and solving interpersonal problems peaceably are important. Problem solving, feeling good about one's efforts, and sticking with a task until it is complete are other important objectives and desired outcomes.

Sample Theme-Based Project

The following is an example of a theme-based activity on "Weather" which is broken down into core content areas of: science and technology, arts, math, social studies and literacy.

WEATHER

Science and Technology

- Design and test a weather vane that measures wind direction.

- Check out an Internet-based, extended weather forecast for your area.

- Study weather maps to see how weather systems travel across the USA.

- Interview a weather forecaster to learn how s/he constructs a forecast.

- Listen to all the weather forecasters for your area. On a given day, how similar are they in their predictions? Note when they all say the same thing about the day. Describe the differences between each forecaster. Who among the forecasters is most accurate on a day to day basis?

- Identify cloud formations by name.

- Keep a chart showing rainfall for a month.

Arts

- Draw a picture that shows a thunderstorm gradually moving into your city.

- Listen to the old song entitled "Stormy Weather." What images does the song bring to mind? Paint, draw or otherwise represent those images visually.

- Visit a local museum to determine which kind of weather (or "bad weather") is most often depicted in the paintings there. (This also relates to data collection and mathematics.)

- Use a variety of brushes and tempera paint to paint a rainstorm.

- Record rain falling on a sidewalk to be listened to as you paint the rainstorm.

Mathematics

- After studying a weather map showing a system of weather moving from west to east across the USA, determine how many days a system takes to reach a certain point.

- How much rain falls into a dish in one rainstorm? How many days does it take to evaporate all the rain collected in a dish once you bring it indoors?

- During a thunderstorm with lightning, measure how many seconds elapse between when you see the lightning and when you hear the thunder?

Social Studies

- At the library, research whether or not Benjamin Franklin really flew a kite in a lightning storm and if so, why.

- Research and deliver a report about tragic weather-related events that have hit your region over the years.

- Look into the evolution of clothing meant to protect people from the rain over the years. Have raincoats changed much in color, design or materials used?

Literacy

- List every word you can think of to talk about the weather.

- Discuss what you think is meant by the saying, "If you don't like the weather now, wait a minute!"

- Sing songs and read stories and poems about the weather.

- Read and discuss the reality of the children's book entitled *Cloudy with a Chance of Meatballs*.

- Take photographs during a field trip during awful weather conditions. Once developed, hang them on a poster-size sheet of paper. For every picture posted, tell the story about what is being depicted, and describe how the viewer might feel if they had been there.

- Write a story that features one *Drop of Water* as the main character. The story can be about a journey this drop took either to the earth or one taken on the earth. For inspiration read *Paddle To The Sea* about a journey a small, handmade canoe takes from north of the Great Lakes to the Atlantic Ocean and beyond.

- Interview someone from the other side of town who experienced the same thunderstorm you did. How were the experiences similar or different?

Project-Based Learning

The key feature of project-based learning activities is "the focus on children's efforts to answer questions that they themselves generate."[28] Most project-based activities are lengthy, and often they require collaboration in a group to be done well. Projects simultaneously expect the project participants to use information they already have while gaining new knowledge and abilities.

Project-based activities provide more intentional and planned learning experiences than play, yet share some of the attractive qualities of play – in the sense that they build on children's interests and are highly engaging for most youth. Project-based activities are especially appropriate for older youth and can be part of a larger, overarching theme your program has selected. You can suggest project topics; however, the best projects are ones generated by the learners as important and relevant for their own individual and personal reasons.

Adults overseeing project-based activities assist in the choosing and planning of the activity based on ideas that come from the children in discussions, especially helping them determine the central questions they are seeking to answer. Staff members locate and provide the materials and tools needed for the project activities, describe the rules associated with involvement in the project and teach the skills each child needs to successfully participate in the activities chosen.

Why Project-Based Learning in After-School Programs?

Children learn to read by reading, compute by computing, solve problems by solving problems and plan by planning and implementing those plans. Project-based activities provide the context and opportunity for children and youth to read, compute, problem solve and plan in pursuit of answers to questions that interest and motivate them.

Generally speaking, most projects allow for problem solving, discussion and finding common ground. In most project-based activities, individuals and groups construct their own learning outcomes. The products generated while doing projects are genuine, student-generated products. Individual and group research is called for in support of the project, and literacy and mathematics concepts are practiced (or learned from direct instruction that is provided as the need becomes apparent) in doing the project.

Project-based activities provide opportunities for individuals to actively use higher level thinking skills to evaluate ideas. Individuals learn to work both autonomously and cooperatively. Many "self-management" experiences and "life experience" skills are practiced and learned. Motivation is generally high because the project direction belongs to the learners involved. The learning that occurs is usually deeper, wider, longer lasting and the result of direct experience. Any direct content instruction – for example, figuring out a fraction – is usually very effective since it serves the learners in very immediate ways.

Section 5

---

[28] From: Worsley, Marilyn, Sallee Beneke, and Judy Harris Helm. "The Pizza Project: Planning and Integrating Math Standards in Project Work." *Young Children*. January 2003.

The immediate and "real world" context means that learning, from one day to the next, is related and built upon. There is usually room for and need for a variety of learning styles and "intelligences" to be applied as various problems or questions get researched, solved and reported.

Time is the greatest challenge of project-based learning. Projects require a team of learners (and staff) who attend the program regularly and are committed to the project over a long period of time. Another challenge is making clear the learning opportunities in project-based learning. Because a project's outcomes are not always as clear cut as those of direct instruction, projects may be considered frivolous by those unfamiliar with the benefits of these kinds of learning experiences.

Good Project Characteristics

Projects should be:

- Stated in an open-ended way. There may be many ways to accomplish the project and many potential outcomes.

- Have well-described variables, boundaries and possible directions.

- Individual or collaborative.

- Stated in such a way that everyone starts off with a sense of how s/he can use skills and understanding s/he already has.

- Shaped by ideas from the learners themselves (and can be sequenced and organized by the adults or the learners).

- A process in which major concepts and learning are *uncovered* not 'covered' by the children and youth.

Project-Based Learning Activity Requirements

When the development, planning, execution, and assessment of a project is truly given to the learners, every project is a unique model unto itself, and generally not repeatable. The age, space and schedule requirements for projects will, therefore, be unique since each project includes different kinds of activities. While there are many unknowns in project-based activities, for projects to be successful many important capabilities must exist. General requirements include:

Of Children and Youth

Socially:

- Be able to listen respectfully to what others are saying in a discussion.

- Be willing to share ideas and findings, some of which might differ from those of others.

- Be willing to abide by the decision-making process and outcome.

- Complete assigned jobs.

- Be willing to collaborate.

Intellectually:

- Be able to read.

- Be able to write and organize information.

- Be able to listen and comprehend what others share.

- Be able to synthesize or put together the bits of information found during research into manageable and related clusters of information.

- Indicate interest for the project topic.

- Be comfortable with and trust his or her construction of knowledge.

Of Leadership

The ability to:

- Determine appropriateness and practicality of topics.

- Locate appropriate project resources and make these resources accessible to children.

- Help break tasks into doable chunks and suggest routes for learners to take to accomplish a task. Help synthesize or combine bits of information.

- Translate or instruct about unfamiliar terms or concepts found during research.

- Help children see how to apply what was researched to the project problem to be solved.

- Model how to share ideas, and applaud respectful sharing and discussions.

- Outline or create a web of an activity including the desired learning outcomes.

- Locate knowledgeable individuals in the community to talk with children and youth about the project topic.

- Ensure that each participant has a role in as many of the project activities and decisions as is appropriate for that individual and his/her interests and skills.

- Document, date, describe and collect enough data to determine the learning outcomes resulting from participation in the project.

- Create a place or opportunity for children and youth to display the products they created or the learning that occurred for them during the project implementation.

Section 5

> **Technology and Project-Based Learning**
>
> The educational philosophy and techniques of project-based, or inquiry-based, learning are particularly well-suited to after-school programs enhanced with technology because they inspire exploration. Moreover, an inquiry-based learning approach is flexible and works well for projects that range from the extensive to the bounded, from the research-oriented to the creative, from the laboratory to the Internet. Finally, an inquiry-based approach validates the experience and knowledge that all kids bring to the learning process. Many kids who have trouble in school because they do not respond well to lectures and memorization will blossom in an inquiry-based learning setting, awakening their confidence, interest, and self-esteem.
>
> — From the YouthLearn Initiative at EDC

Project Phases

Phase I: *Beginning the Project*

- Brainstorm a topic to investigate.
- Develop a "Know? Want to Know? Learn" (K-W-L) chart. (See Appendix B.)
- Explore various aspects of the topic, e.g. hands-on activities with tools, artifacts, ingredients, drawing, construction, pretend play.
- Develop a planning web which anticipates the concepts that children might learn in their topic investigations (e.g. pizza restaurants, kinds of pizzas, pizza ingredients, process for making, delivery, etc.) (See Out of Doors Web and Track Meet Web.)
- Link to learning standards by identifying the core curriculum areas that most naturally connect. (This may be done separately by adults. See Section 4.)

Phase II: *Investigation*

- Decide on some aspect of the topic to be investigated.
- Invite an expert to discuss the topic, or arrange a field trip to a place where the topic can be investigated. Beforehand, generate a list of what children and youth would anticipate seeing or learning.
- Decide on the "L" (what was learned), and what else (the "W") could be learned in a second visit or discussion.
- Sketch, draw, photograph, describe, interview, count and record the investigation.
- Decide on what to do next or with the information or knowledge.
- Do whatever is decided.
- Keep a record of experiences and learning.

Phase III: *Concluding the Project*

- Conduct appropriate culminating activity in which children can demonstrate what they have learned (e.g. presentation, party, exhibition, fair, video, etc.) Determine expenses, amounts, materials, space, and schedule for this event.
- Reflect on learning for individuals/group using K-W-L chart and on expected outcomes.

Sample Project-Based Activities

1. **"Sleeping Bag Project"** involves designing, assembling, and distributing sleeping bags for homeless people. Some of the things youth involved in this project may experience:

    - The physical, social and emotional experience of actually making the bags.
    - The establishment of rituals associated with packaging the bags and the interpersonal experience of giving them away to someone.
    - The design experience involving studying homelessness as a concept, measuring the users to determine optimal sizes, studying the materials that can easily, and cost effectively be used to make the bag.

2. **"Honoring Historical Teens Project"** Teenagers identify and research teenagers who played a significant, but unsung or unrecognized, part in improving the lives of the people in your town.

    - Collect photographs; interview surviving relatives, interview surviving (now adult) teens.
    - Create a dialogue, to accompany a Ken Burns-style video/documentary of those teen's lives.

3. **"Time Capsule Project"** What do children and youth want the world 100 years from now to know about teens and children in the current year? Children and youth bury a capsule filled with objects that they think best represent childhood/ teen-hood in the 21st century, or a theme of choice. Press coverage should be encouraged and the formal burial site should be as public as possible.

4. **Interviewing the elderly** to collect, document, record and publish "old time" ways of doing things.

5. **Run a 'sand castle building contest'** event on a public beach or by bringing sand into the program.

6. **Set up a cookie factory** to make and sell cookies and learn basic economics.

Additional Project-Based Learning Resources

1. **Buck Institute for Education** (BIE) specializes in Project-Based Learning training opportunities. They also publish the Project Based Learning Handbook, which guides leaders through project planning and implementation stages. **www.bie.org**

2. **The Global Schoolhouse** brings together opportunities for conducting projects using the Internet and working collaboratively with schools across the world. It contains a project registry with over 900 online projects and conducts an annual competition among schools and youth organizations around the world to conduct research and publish their findings on the Web. **www.globalschoolnet.org/index.html**

3. **The International Education and Resource Network** (iEARN) is a non-profit global network that enables young people to use the Internet and other new technologies to engage in collaborative educational projects that both enhance learning and make a difference in the world. Participants may join existing structured online projects, or work with others internationally to create and facilitate their own projects to fit their own particular classroom and curriculum needs. **www.iearn.org**

4. **PBLNet.org** In addition to exemplary projects created by Project-Based Learning (PBL) educators, this site has an extensive list of resources and research findings on PBL including assessment and standards. Designed for use by educators and parents. **www.pblnet.org**

5. **The Project Approach** offers professional development, self-study courses and resources for learning about project-based instruction in elementary classrooms. **www.project-approach.com/default.htm**

6. **ThinkQuest** is an international competition where student teams engage in collaborative, project-based learning to create educational websites. The winning entries form the ThinkQuest online library that contains links to over 5,000 student-created sites. **www.thinkquest.org**

7. **The YouthLearn Initiative** at Education Development Center features lesson plans, techniques and tips on curriculum design, and other resources for learning programs, with an emphasis on project-based learning and technology integration. In addition to the website and The YouthLearn Guide, YouthLearn also offers a database of additional resources and a discussion list for youth development practitioners. **www.youthlearn.org**

Recommended Reading

1. Helm, J.H. and Lillian Katz. *Young Investigators: The Project Approach in the Early Years*. New York: Teachers College Press. 2001.

2. Helm, J.H. and S. Beneke, (Eds.). *The Power of Projects - Meeting contemporary challenges in early childhood classrooms - Strategies and Solutions*. New York: Teachers College Press. 2002.

3. Katz, Lillian, & S.C. Chard, *Engaging Children's Minds: The Project Approach*. Norwood, NJ: Ablex. 1989.

Section 5

Discussion Questions for Section Five

1. Think back on your own experiences in school, camp or after-school programs. Try to recall when the experiences you had were organized under a thematic title or as in-depth projects. Share your thoughts about what happened, and the effectiveness of these themes/projects in organizing the activities that occurred.

2. List some themes/projects you think would be good for organizing activities at your after-school program. Why did you choose these particular activities?

NOTES

Links to Learning: *A Curriculum Planning Guide for After-School Programs*

Section Six:

Key Learning Areas

Literacy
- Why Include Literacy Activities in After-School Programs?
- Activities that Support Literacy Development
- Environment
- Daily Schedule
- Age and Development
- Sample Literacy Activity Plan
- Linking to Quality Standards and Learning Benchmarks
- Other Sample Literacy Activities
- Additional Literacy Resources

Science
- Why Include Science in After-School Programs?
- Recognizing the Science Moment
- Environment
- Daily Schedule
- Age and Development
- Sample Science Activity Plan
- Linking to Quality Standards and Learning Benchmarks
- Other Sample Science Activities
- Additional Science Resources

Math Problem Solving
- Why Include Math Problem-Solving Activities in After-School?
- Real Child Solutions
- Mathematics as a Descriptive Language
- Mathematics: Concepts and Operations
- Occasions for Problem Solving and Using Math Language
- Sample Math Problem Solving Activity Plan
- Linking to Quality Standards and Learning Benchmarks
- Other Sample Math Problem-Solving Activities
- Additional Math Problem-Solving Resources

Arts Curriculum
- Why Include Arts in After-School Programs?
- What Can Children and Youth Learn from Art?
- Environment

- Daily Schedule
- Age and Development
- Sample Arts Activity Plan
- Linking to Quality Standards and Learning Benchmarks
- Other Sample Arts Activities
- Additional Arts Resources

Social Competence
- Why Include Social-Competence Activities in After-School Programs?
- What Can Children and Youth Learn from Social-Competence Activities?
- Environment
- Daily Schedule
- Social Competence of Caregivers
- Age and Development
- Sample Social Competence Activity Plan
- Linking to Quality Standards and Learning Benchmarks
- Other Sample Social-Competence Activities
- Additional Social-Competence Resources

Fitness and Nutrition
- Why Include Fitness and Nutrition in After-School Programs?
- What Can Children and Youth Learn from Fitness and Nutrition Activities?
- Three Fitness and Nutrition Concepts
- Age and Development
- Daily Schedule
- Sample Fitness Activity Plan
- Linking to Quality Standards and Learning Benchmarks
- Additional Fitness and Nutrition Resources

Technology
- Why Include Technology in After-School Programs?
- Integrating Technology Effectively
- Environment
- Daily Schedule
- Age and Development
- Sample Technology Activity Plan
- Linking to Quality Standards and Learning Benchmarks
- Other Sample Technology Activities
- Additional Technology Resources

Section Six
Key Learning Areas

In striving to increase out-of-school-time learning supports, after-school programs often select certain subject areas on which to concentrate. The chosen subjects will depend on many different factors including the core expertise of the after-school provider agency, the strengths and interests of the staff and the needs and interests of the students. This Guide focuses on the following seven "key learning areas" and provides sample activity plans and additional resources for each one.

1. **Literacy**
2. **Science**
3. **Math Problem Solving**
4. **Arts**
5. **Social Competence**
6. **Fitness and Nutrition**
7. **Technology**

In a typical after-school program, it is recommended that activities associated with key learning areas be embedded into the overall schedule, balanced throughout the day and week. For example:

Free Time: The child can choose among several activities that incorporate specific learning areas.

Examples:

Literacy Development: children and youth can choose:

- To read quietly.

- To describe with words – either orally or in writing – an object in a "mystery box."

Science: children and youth can choose:

- To make gliders from index cards.

- To solve the "What is making holes in the tree on the playground?" problem.

Small Group or Individual

Examples:

- Math problem solving: Children and youth will attempt to figure out how many chairs will be needed if every child's parents come to the meeting that night.

- Technology/Arts: Youth go online to find information relating to a project on costume design.

Large Group

Examples:

▪ Fitness: participate in a physical activity such as soccer, basketball or Frisbee™.

▪ Nutrition: Participate in taste test of healthy snack options.

Indoors or Outdoors

Example:

▪ Arts/Social Competence: children and youth do "chalk drawing" on the sidewalk to demonstrate an alternative to local graffiti artists who have vandalized a neighborhood wall.

For simplicity and clarity in this Guide, each "key learning area" is addressed as a separate subject. However, as will quickly become apparent, many activities – particularly project-based ones – combine multiple learning areas.

The activity plans provided here are designed as starting points; they are not intended to be exhaustive or proscriptive. Likewise, the templates that link activities to learning benchmarks and quality standards are provided as samples of how a program might apply local standards to a given activity. Finally, the additional resources sections contain just a sampling of the many activities, materials and organizations that exist and can aid your curriculum planning efforts.

Literacy

Literacy develops through reading, writing, speaking and listening. Literacy also includes gathering information, using information, thinking critically, understanding others, and expressing one's self through the use of language. Language – both written and oral – serves a variety of purposes. It is a:

- Source of information (books, lectures, schedules, menus, rules).

- Source of pleasure or recreation (conversation, discussions, magazines, newspapers).

- Means of recording, or keeping track of things we find important or may need to reference at a later date (observations, experiences, events).

- Way to communicate information, thoughts, feelings and needs to others (letters, articles, essays, stories, messages, requests).

Why Include Literacy Activities in After-School Programs?

Among adults with very low literacy skills, 43 percent live in poverty and 70 percent have no job or a part-time job. Among children who have difficulty reading, 15 percent drop out of high school and only 2 percent earn a degree from a four-year college. Helping children and youth develop strong literacy skills can reduce their chances of being reflected in these sobering statistics as they grow up.

Children who learn to read easily are usually provided with positive expectations about literacy at an early age. After-school programs that provide quality experiences in reading, writing and communicating can create these positive expectations without necessarily teaching reading or writing.

Activities that Support Literacy Development

Literacy development is more than just reading. According to experts in the field, the following activities, many of which already occur in after-school programs, also support literacy development in children and youth in very important ways.[29]

Holding conversations with children and adults

The act of talking to another person is a way to hear new words and learn new things. Good listeners "tell" the speaker that s/he has interesting and important things to say.

> **Examples:** "Tell me about your weekend. What was special?"
>
> "Hey, I notice you have a new jacket. Is it warm/your favorite color/on sale?" etc.
>
> "Let me introduce you to my friend. This is ____. She's from _____."

---

[29] Adapted from: Hynes, K., S. O'Connor and A.M. Chung, "Literacy: Exploring Strategies to Enhance Learning in After-school Programs", Wellesley: National Institute on Out-of-School Time, The M.O.S.T Initiative. 1999.

Helping children and youth follow their interests

Reading, writing and speaking are done willingly when the person is interested in the topic or expects to gain something from the effort. Listening to what children and youth want to share about a book they just read is an important way to keep up with what they are thinking about or are interested in. It's also a way to validate their thinking or opinions, and it opens up an opportunity for them to ask questions.

Examples:

"I was noticing how interested you were in the birds at the feeder yesterday, so I took this book of birds out of the library for you to use to identify the birds that come to eat."

"John, would you be willing to answer that question for Jason? You know more about dinosaurs than I do."

"Why don't you write (for the program newspaper) your opinion about the new neighborhood project. I liked your thoughts."

Taking field trips

Experiences at museums, public gardens and historical sites become adventures to talk, write or read about, especially if these are new places for children.

Examples:

Make a list of everything in a nearby city you want to see. Devise a timetable for visiting. Create a visitor's diary for recording your impressions. Share your journey with a parent group. Write thank you notes to museum personnel who were helpful. Make oral presentations to friends who were unable to go on the trip. Research the history associated with a site.

"If you are interested in knowing more about the story depicted in the monument we visited, here is a book on it."

"The airplane we visited has an interesting history associated with it. Did you know its first pilot was a woman?"

"Here's a book of photographs showing the changes in the harbor over the last 300 years."

Reading stories aloud

After reading a book aloud, instead of asking abstract questions meant to satisfy some reading comprehension skills, ask, "What does this story make you think about?" or "How did this story make you feel?" Hearing a story read aloud allows students to experience the sounds that words and letters have and match their own images with the words.

Example: Read aloud each day at a regular time, e.g. during snack time, at transitions between activities, at the opening or closing of each day. Use the book to start a conversation or discussion.

Problem-solving experiences

People invariably talk to each other and to themselves in problem-solving situations. Talking is good practice for choosing words, creating thoughts and hearing feedback from others. Hearing or reading a problem requires effort at understanding. Again, language skills are learned largely by way of association with other people; in a collaborative project, children are required to talk, negotiate and explain things to each other.

Examples:
Crossword puzzles, fill-in-the-blank, putting story parts in sequence, writing or brainstorming aloud an alternative ending to a story are examples of problem-solving experiences that get students to use language in challenging ways.

Speaking and listening experiences

Speaking and interpreting a language (talking, listening to and understanding when others talk) are largely learned by experiencing them on a day-by-day basis. Very little formal instruction goes into enabling children to speak and listen well in their earliest years. The more one speaks and is asked to listen, the better one gets at being able to do those things. Children raised in a situation where language experiences are limited are frequently delayed in their language development.

Examples: Snack-time conversations, singing or rhyming games, listening to music or someone explaining the music.

Computer skill learning

Word processing programs can make writing and editing much easier than writing by hand. Storing, retrieving, revising and sending one's writing around the globe are inspiring, exciting prospects. The ease associated with these options can motivate young writers, since the computer performs much of the labor.

Examples:
Having pen pals, writing, retrieving, editing and storing written work in computer data-bases, reading about or listening to others talk about new software and writing to others to share new technology information all develop language proficiency.

Exposure to music, dance and arts performances

When experiences involving the arts move from being just entertaining and begin to be used to educate and inform the children who attend, then reading, listening, writing, gathering information and using new insights gained from that exposure support the development of literacy.

Examples:
Reading about the artists, interviewing the artists, attending a pre-performance lecture and attending a documentary film presentation on the piece of art and its development.

Environment

The physical environment children and youth spend time in contributes quietly, but enormously, to their literacy development. We are surrounded everyday of our lives with printed and oral language. They play a huge role in our language learning and are resources for living a safe, full and enjoyable life. They label, explain, give direction, entertain and inform us about very important things such as where to sit, what to do, which way is the wrong way, which lavatory for one's gender, what to expect, etc. Language, in all its forms, provides us with a variety of ways to think about many issues of importance.

Reading, writing and listening experiences generally require print-rich but quiet, well-lit spaces with comfortable places to sit. A wide range of literature should be available, representing a variety of reading levels. These should be easily accessible by children and youth, encouraging them to make relevant choices based on their interests.

Paper, pencils, pens, writing surfaces, dictionaries, a direct light source, perhaps computers, audio-visual software and machines such as tape recorders, CD players and video players represent the basic space and materials required for implementing a literacy program. Ideally there should also be props for creative dramatics, musical instruments for making story-related music, crayons, markers, paint, glue sticks and collage materials to make book posters or to imitate favorite book illustrators and letter paper and envelopes for writing to favorite authors or illustrators.

Key Ingredients in a Language-Rich Environment

1. *Adults and peers model, encourage and enable the development of literacy abilities by regularly reading, writing, speaking and listening.*

Witnessing others participating in real and engaging reading, writing, speaking and listening does a lot to encourage literacy development in general. Nothing in the entire after-school program day has more impact in convincing children and youth that books and language abilities are worthwhile than the example set by the program's adults. As adults begin to appreciate the power of enriching, entertaining and informing themselves, their ability to develop language abilities in others grows.

2. *Reading Centers have a wide variety of books on display and the books are easily accessible.*

To catch children and youth's attention, a wide variety of books, in different formats, need to be available all the time: picture, chapter, illustrated, audio-taped, fiction, non-fiction, poetry, and at all different levels of difficulty. Children and youth can make their own choices of books to read; no stigma or value is attached to the type of books selected by individuals. Adult leaders can read books aloud each day and introduce specific books to children whom the leader knows might be interested. There should be sufficient time available in the daily schedule for reading to take place. A Reading Center can have shelves for books, pillows, comfortable chairs or couches, "homey" lamps and furnishings that invite reading to occur. Reading Centers should be quiet places, separate from the noisier activities of the program.

3. *Decorations, hanging posters, artwork and other displays "advertise" certain books or encourage children and youth to investigate themes or topics.*

These consistent and sincere invitations are provided in hopes that the child or youth will relate to what they see and hear and begin to read, write, speak or listen to others as they share their experiences. Posters featuring child-appropriate movies based on books (for example, *Harry Potter* or *Lord of the Rings*) might lead some youth to want to read the book. Displays of Native American-inspired artifacts might encourage interest in books about Native Americans. Children's attempts to use the illustration techniques in certain children's books might lead them to notice and read books by those authors.

4. *Staff provide steady recommendations to encourage children and youth to read certain books.*

Frequent readers are always anticipating and looking forward to reading their next book, even before finishing the one they are on. They are eager to share ideas and talk to others about the books they are reading. The talk may not always be about how wonderful a book is, but it can include their frustrations, dislikes or concerns about the book's content, language, structure or themes. If children and youth read or listen to a book they favor and think others would enjoy, they can be encouraged to develop "commercials" – drawn, written, or acted out – to encourage others to read or hear the recommended book.

5. *Writing areas are established where a wide variety of writing tools and materials are available.*

Readily available writing tools and paper and places to write comfortably will enable writing to occur. The Writing Center can be associated with the Reading Center, but it doesn't have to be. New colored pencils, fancy pens with interesting colored inks, interesting writing papers and pads, as well as lap-held writing tablets or lighted tables can draw children in if for no other reason than trying them out. Examples of child-centered writing activities include: re-writing the ending to a favorite book, drawing the map which describes the setting of a story or developing a "commercial" for a favorite book.

Acquiring Books and Setting up a Lending Library

Ideas for acquiring books include:

- Borrow them from the local school or public library.

- Ask children and youth to bring them from home on loan.

- Buy books at yard sales, used bookstores or from those taken out of circulation by the local library. (Damaged, dirty, out-dated or donated editions of books are sold for pennies at most libraries.)

- Book Clubs such as Trumpet, Scholastic, Troll, or Weekly Reader sell books for a dollar or two. Each month the club's catalog of books arrives with order blanks enough for each child to take home or for the center to use in purchasing its own copies of best selling paperback books for children and youth.

- "Birthday Books" are books purchased by parents but given to the program to celebrate each child's birthday.

- "Book Drives" are opportunities for local citizens to contribute unwanted books to the after-school program. They need to be sorted for content and appropriateness for the levels of reading ability found in your site. Duplicates or inappropriate books can be sold to make money for purchasing new books.

Once a library is set up, the leaders need to decide if books can only be read in the program site, or can be taken home and read. If they can be checked out, a system for tracking books needs to be set up. Determine how long a book can circulate, the fines associated with late returns, and a way to show which books are in house and which are out.

Daily Schedule

Any literacy development program requires a regular and dedicated place in the daily schedule, either during free choice time or as a group activity. Reading aloud to others or quietly to oneself begins with having had ample time to select a book to read. Follow-up experiences such as discussions about the story, writing an alternative ending, or arts and crafts experiences related to the story, take time to unfold. Provide enough time in the schedule for varied literacy development experiences.

Age and Development

As an adult you can introduce books based on what you know about children's interests and abilities. You can interview children and youth to find out what they want to read about. When given a chance to choose books on their own, children generally choose books that are at, or just below, their reading abilities. That's okay since after-school programs are not generally in the business of teaching new reading skills; they are instead aimed at helping children practice and learn to enjoy reading.

 Links to Learning: *A Curriculum Planning Guide for After-School Programs*

Making the Kid to Book Link

Inspiring long-lasting responses to books by children and youth begins with your enthusiasm about books, your interest in children's book interests and the quality of the activities that emerge from those books.

Children Choose Books:

- That were recommended or read aloud to them.

- That were included in an attractive display or had appealing illustrations.

- That came recommended by peers.

- That are about things they are interested in.

How Children Read Books:

- Some children notice artistic styles and 'signatures' or details in the illustrations.

- Some children skim the book, rapidly looking at each page, then return to the beginning to look closer.

- Many early readers look at the illustrations before looking at the words, looking to the pictures to help them out if they get stuck on a word or phrase.

- More skilled readers go right to the words and refer to the illustrations to look for the objects, characters, settings or situations described by the words.

Section 6

Sample Literacy Activity Plan

Title

Guide to the City/Neighborhood/Community

Description

Engage children and youth in exploration of city/neighborhood/community and create a written guide to share their learning with others.

Objectives

Provide literacy, fitness, social competence and arts activities.

Intended Outcomes

- Children and youth will gain experience and practice reading, writing, speaking and listening.
- Children and youth will participate in outdoor exploration that will contribute to their physical fitness.
- Children and youth will broaden their understanding of their community and the perspectives of others in their group.
- Children and youth will express their new understanding/ knowledge through a variety of media such as writing, drawing, painting, singing, acting, etc.

Special Materials and Tools

Large chart paper and markers, maps of the area, sample guide books, historical books about the area, books about cities, bulletin boards, tape recorder/tapes, library and/or Internet access, blank book for final guide.

Space Requirements

Discussion space, tables to work at/write on, storage for ongoing project materials, a stage or performing space.

Age/Group Size

Appropriate for ages 10 and up. This project could involve a lot of children and youth or just a few. If many children participate, divide into small groups (3-4) for different components.

The Activity

1. Survey children's existing knowledge of the city/neighborhood in small discussion groups. Pose questions which invite children to both share and reveal their knowledge and preconceptions about 1) cities/towns as a concept (functions, services, public and private spaces, shapes, boundaries and inhabitants); 2) your specific city/town (children's direct experiences, multi-sensory perceptions and opinions).

2. Create a Guide to the City/Neighborhood/Community. Discuss "What is a guide?" and "Who is the audience for this guide?" (pictures or maps, someone who knows the city, an object or tool for supporting curiosity, knowledge, information, a tool for exploring, finding novelty, surprise or pleasure.) Inventory, describe, make maps, etc.

3. Select the maps, drawings and transcribed anecdotes created and shared during the course of the project that best meet the guide's purpose and put them together in a blank book suitable for mounting and organizing the guide ingredients.

Incorporating Technology

- Use Internet search tools to find information about the community.
- View sample "guides" online to generate ideas.
- Develop web pages to create "online" version of guide.

Extensions and Continuations

- Create a play or song about the city/community.
- Organize walking tours for other children or parents.

Conclusions/Reflections

Hold discussion with children and youth about what they learned about their community. Have them write to their parents or elected officials about what they learned.

Documentation

The written guide book, any maps children and youth create, bulletin board displays, videotapes or audiotapes of any related presentations/ performances by the children, photographs of stages of the project.

Section 6

Linking to Quality Standards and Learning Benchmarks

Activity Title	Guide to the City/Neighborhood/Community						
Description	Engage children and youth in exploration of city/neighborhood/community and create a written guide to share their learning with others.						

Core Content Area (check all that apply)	Math	Literacy	Science	Arts	Fitness/ Nutrition	Social Competence	Other
		✓		✓	✓	✓	

Skills for the New Economy (check all that apply)	Numeracy	Communication		Problem solving	Technology	Work w/others
		✓		✓	✓	✓

Quality Standards	**NAA** #4 – Staff interact with children to help them learn #14 – Activities reflect the mission of the program and promote the development of all children #25 – Builds links to the community #28 – Staff and children work together to plan suitable activities	**SACERS** 20. Arts and Crafts 24. Language/ reading activities 27. Cultural awareness	**OTHER** Search Institute's 40 Developmental Assets #22 – young person actively engaged in learning

	Standard	Grade/Age	Description
Benchmark or Learning Standard	Checkpoints for Progress in Literacy	Third Sixth	· Read for fun, information and understanding · Put together thoughts and information in writing · Connect ideas and information in reading with real life experiences · Edit work to create final product
Benchmark or Learning Standard	CASEL Social Emotional Learning Competencies	N/A	Social awareness: appreciating diversity Relationship skills: communication, building relationships, negotiation
Benchmark or Learning Standard	Massachusetts Learning Standards for the Arts	N/A	Production and performance: use the arts as a way of expressing ideas, feelings and beliefs.
Benchmark or Learning Standard	National Content Standards for Physical Education	K-12	#3 – Exhibits physically active lifestyle #7 – Understands that physical activity provides opportunities for enjoyment and social interaction.

Other Sample Literacy Activities

1. Re-write a story, telling it from the point of view of a different character. Example: The grandmother or the woodcutter in *Little Red Riding Hood*, rather than Little Red Riding Hood herself. (Ages 8-10)

2. Turn stories into news. For example, write a newspaper headline or an imaginary interview for a main character or object in a story, as if you had arrived at that moment as a local TV reporter. (Ages 10-12)

3. Have children try using words – orally and in writing – to describe a familiar place or activity (e.g. their home or making a peanut butter and jelly sandwich). See if their peers can follow their descriptions to draw a floor plan or make the sandwich. (Ages 12-14)

4. Arts and Crafts:
   a. Make a diorama of an important scene in a book. (Ages 8-10)
   b. Draw "Reward" posters of main characters with enough description of their characteristics to make it easy for people to recognize them. (Ages 6-8)
   c. Design a new dust jacket or poster for a favorite book. (Ages 6-16)
   d. Make a picture, poster, or book cover using the same illustration style and medium (pen, watercolors, collage, prints, etc.) of the book's illustrator. (Ages 6-16)
   e. Design a 'coat-of-arms' for a principal character in a story. (Ages 8-16)

5. Make a game board and game, using plots, scenes and characters from a story. (Ages 9-12)

6. Act out the action in a story or poem (e.g. *Casey At The Bat*, *The Three Billy Goats Gruff*). (Ages 7-10)

Additional Literacy Resources

1. **After-School.gov** website provides information about federal programs that support children and youth during out-of-school hours. The Planning Activities page points to numerous sites that have great ideas for activities under different topics including "Reading and Writing." **www.after-school.gov**

2. **America Reads** is a national campaign of the U.S. Department of Education promoting the involvement of every American in ensuring child literacy. To join the America Reads Listserv, email majordomo@etr-associates.org, type in body of message: subscribe americareads. **www.ed.gov/inits/americareads**

3. **Between the Lions, Get Wild About Reading!** This popular early literacy program on public television has numerous resources for teachers and parents to assist with literacy development. **http://pbskids.org/lions/**

Section 6

4. **Book Adventure** is a free, online reading motivation program for children in grades K-8. Children create their own book lists from over 6,000 recommended titles, take multiple choice quizzes on the books they've read offline and earn points and prizes for their literary successes. **www.bookadventure.org/index.asp**

5. **Centro para el Estudio de Libros Infantiles y Juveniles en Español (Center for the Study of Books in Spanish for Children and Adolescents)** A bilingual website promoting Spanish literacy. Includes 5,500 recommended Spanish-language books and many other resources. **www.csusm.edu/csb/**

6. **KidzLit** is an after-school curriculum designed to build reading fun and social skills through story guides, games and group activities. **www.kidzafterschool.org**

7. **National Center for Family Literacy** works with educators and community builders to design and sustain family literacy programs that meet the urgent educational needs of disadvantaged families. **www.famlit.org/Resources/index.cfm**

8. **Northwest Regional Educational Laboratory** provides an online selection of games and activities using letters and words that give children another way to integrate their learning and reinforce their literacy skills. **www.nwrel.org/learns/trainingopps/games/index.html**

9. **Reading is Fundamental (RIF)** is the nation's largest non-profit children's literacy organization that runs numerous literacy programs especially targeted to children in communities of greatest economic need. **www.rif.org**

10. **Resource Books to Promote Literacy**:
    - *50 Fantastic Poems With Wonderful Writing Prompts: Using Thought-Provoking Prompts to Get Kids Writing, Writing, Writing*
    - *25 Mini-Lessons for Teaching Writing: Quick Lessons That Help Students Become Effective Writers*
    - *The Big Book of Ready-to-Go Writing Lessons: 50 Engaging Activities With Graphic Organizers That Teach Kids How to Tell a Story, Convey Information, Describe, Persuade and More!*

    Available through an online bookseller or: **http://teacher.scholastic.com/ professional/profbooks/index.htm**

11. **The Spaghetti Book Club** website contains book reviews by kids and for kids, searchable by title, author and reviewer (identified only by first name and last initial). Some reviews include original artwork. Any student, class or after-school group can join and will get their own web page. **www.spaghettibookclub.org**

Recommended Reading

1. **Guide to Literacy for Volunteers and Tutors** is online at the Bank Street College website: **www.bankstreet.edu/literacyguide**

2. **Learning to Read - Resources for Language Arts and Reading Research** This website serves as a clearinghouse for the dissemination of reading research through conferences, journals and other publications, primarily a list of links and book reviews on topics such as literacy, interactive lessons and professional publications. **http://toread.com**

3. **Literacy - Teaching in the Language Arts** has an extensive list of links to information about multiple topics related to literacy in children. The site offers links to lists of prize-winning books, spelling and grammar sites and others. **http://falcon.jmu.edu/~ramseyil/literacy.htm**

4. **On the Road to Reading: A Guide for Community Partners** gives examples of successful tutoring/literacy programs and suggestions for program design. It also describes the process of how children learn language and contains an extensive section on other literacy resources. **www.ed.gov/pubs/RoadtoRead/**

5. **The Reading First** initiative builds on the findings of years of scientific research to ensure that more children receive effective reading instruction in the early grades. This website provides excellent background reading and research on literacy. **www.ed.gov/programs/readingfirst/resources.html**

6. **Tips for Promoting Reading and Literacy in Out-of-School Time Programs for Children.** See pages 11-13 of this NIOST publication for an overview of how to promote reading and literacy in out-of-school programs. **http://www.niost.org/publications/promoting.pdf**

Science

Science is at the heart of human curiosity, asking questions and finding answers. Project-based activities in after-school programs are among the best places for children and youth to explore and learn about science. Comprehending science means understanding:

- How a variety of things in the world work.
- How the choices we make about the earth affect the quality of life for others.
- How information and knowledge come from studying and researching the world around us.
- The history of science and technology that informs our knowledge today.

Engineering is about applying science to design and manufacture inventions, devices, robots or machines that make life easier. Technology is often coupled with engineering. Computers are an example of engineering and technology applied to the issues of writing, communicating, retrieving, storing and locating information.

Why Include Science in After-School Programs?

By increasing children and youth's interest in and exposure to science, after-school programs can help children develop a host of skills that will help them understand and thrive in the world around them. Through science, they will learn:

- How to find out about the world.
- How to observe and record: keeping records of what was seen or heard.
- How to plan, implement and interpret results of experimentation.
- How to communicate ideas and findings: telling others what you learned.
- Tool and instrument use: microscopes, eyedroppers, compasses, balance scales, tweezers, binoculars, telescopes, cameras, etc.

Recognizing the Science Moment

Offering science activities is a good way to help children and youth learn science. However, recognizing that science is happening all around us is an equally valid way to think about science in after-school programs. As an after-school provider, think of your role as one of alerting children and youth to anything unfamiliar or curious about the physical world. This can be done by bringing into the program artifacts and examples of the biological and physical world for children and youth to explore and examine, or by bringing in experts in various scientific fields to talk with or do projects with your group. Modeling your curiosity about the physical world and science often gives children the permission and validation they might need to be inquisitive.

For many after-school programs, especially those that don't set up "science time" or "science clubs," many occasions for science will arise in the normal course of a regular day.

- During an athletic event: determining which part of your foot kicks the soccer ball further.
- On a walk: stopping to study ants as they move in and out of their ant holes.
- While cooking or preparing snacks: studying the "wedge structure and seed numbers" of different citrus fruits by looking for differences and similarities.
- Looking out the window: watching a thunderstorm, noting temperature changes, wind direction and thunder/lightning time relationships.
- Watching a bird build a nest, identifying the bird and the nest-making materials, keeping track of how long it takes to build the nest and when eggs are laid and hatched, and noting when the chicks fledge and leave the nest.

Occasions such as these are important times for you to recognize the science learning potential and implement one or more of the following scientific methods:

- Observe what's happening, record what is observed, use the tools of the scientist to deepen that observation, plan and implement an experiment to see if your ideas are valid, interpret the results, conclude and share findings with others who might be interested.
- Bring in experts in a field of science children are interested in or provide opportunities for them to apprentice with real scientists.
- Let children and youth become familiar with how things feel, look or work.
- Create observational drawings while closely studying something of interest or graphically record the changes in something over time.
- Discuss and argue your opinion about something others are studying (e.g. global warming, greenhouse emissions, mercury-levels in fish) as scientists do at science conferences.
- Test to determine the qualities of something (e.g. strength, absorbency, taste or shelf life).
- Set up a competition to inspire discovery and experimentation (e.g. designing the perfect long-range glider).

Environment

The success of any science activity is dependent on having the right space for each kind of activity. Science activities are best done in an area designated for science. Messy activities require spaces and surfaces that can be easily cleaned. Accessing reference materials needs good light and a quiet environment. Group work requires a large space and work surface. In general, the best kinds of science activities for after-school programs are active or hands-on: children and youth are busy making things, trying out ideas, testing understandings and checking in with each other's activities.

Section 6

Outdoor space requirements differ depending on the activity being done. If the children are launching model rockets, then a huge safe space separate from the general public is required. On the other hand, if children are studying how robins find worms, then the activity will require robins, worms, a lawn and a spot from which to observe. Pond water study needs a pond, tide pool studies need an ocean environment and star study needs a night-time setting free from city lights.

Daily Schedule

Science activities generally need a regularly scheduled and extended period of time for children to get involved in meaningful ways. Allow enough time for the participants to get invested in an experience and then let it run for 30 minutes longer. When activities are cut short just as youth are on the verge of a discovery or before they get a chance to test their ideas, they learn not to take the activity too seriously. Also having to wait too long between related activities can diminish children's interest. Lengthy science projects can be introduced during free choice time so those who are interested can stay involved and those who are ready to move on can do so.

Age and Development

Most science activity plans will provide a suggested age, however, some activities that specify older youth can be done well by certain younger children who have the desire and appropriate skills. One rule of thumb for determining developmental appropriateness is to analyze what are called the "activity requirements" of every activity. Does the child/youth have the skills, strength, information, desire and supportive resources necessary to successfully participate? If the child has only some of the requirements, are there adults or knowledgeable peers who can assist the child where necessary? If the answer is yes, then the activity might be appropriate and successful. This kind of situation will be a true and valid learning experience for the child. If children know everything they need to know in order to be successful in the experience, then it is perfectly appropriate to invite them to do it.

Sample Science Activity Plan

Title
Amusement Park for Birds

Description
Design and build an amusement park for summer birds based on observations of bird behavior near a winter feeder.

Objectives
Provide long-term, hands-on science activity that incorporates literacy, fitness/nutrition and social competence learning opportunities.

Intended Outcomes
- Children will gain understanding of wildlife, environment, weather, simple mechanics and physics and other aspects of the physical world.
- Children will participate in outdoor exploration and physical activities that will contribute to their physical fitness and understanding of nutrition.
- Children will gain experience working with others to gain understanding and solve problems.
- Children will gain experience and practice reading, writing, speaking and listening.

Special Materials and Tools
Birdfeeder (or materials to construct a birdfeeder), birdseed, writing and drawing materials, simple construction materials – paper, cardboard, plastic, wood – to make "amusements," camera.

Space Requirements
Outdoor space to locate birdfeeder and amusement part. Indoor space for discussions, writing, drawing and storage.

Age/Group Size
Appropriate for ages 9-12. Could involve many children or just a few. Need children with long-term commitment/involvement.

The Activity
Phase One (winter): Discussion: find out what children know about birds – what they eat, what they like to do, etc. Introduce birdfeeder idea and engage them in designing, constructing or positioning feeder. Observe birds and their activities and record observations. Read about the birds that show up.

Phase Two (spring/summer): Discussion: why aren't birds coming to the feeder any more? What can we do to attract birds back to our space? Observe birds in local park. Read/research more about birds. Construct "amusements" to attract birds. Record observations.

Incorporating Technology

- Use Internet to find information about local birds and their habitats, activities, etc.
- Take photos or video of project stages and create multimedia presentation.

Extensions and Continuations

There are many possible arts-related extensions of this activity. Children can make drawings/paintings/photographs of the birds in the amusement park. Or they could write stories/poems/songs about the birds.

Conclusions/Reflections

Hold discussion with children about what they learned about birds, comparisons with their own "amusements" and those of birds. What did they learn about working together, solving problems, etc.

Documentation

Book of observations about the birds, the birdfeeder/amusements, photographs of the different bird activities/seasons.

Linking to Quality Standards and Learning Benchmarks

Activity Title	Amusement Park for Birds						
Description	Design and build an amusement park for summer birds based on observations of bird behavior near a winter feeder.						

Core Content Area (check all that apply)	Math	Literacy	Science	Arts	Fitness/ Nutrition	Social Competence	Other
		✓	✓		✓	✓	

Skills for the New Economy (check all that apply)	Numeracy	Communication		Problem solving	Technology	Work w/others
		✓		✓	✓	✓

Quality Standards	**NAA** #4 – Staff interact with children to help them learn #13 – Children can choose from a variety of activities #15 – There are sufficient materials to support program activities #28 – Staff and children work together to plan suitable activities	**SACERS** 22. Blocks and construction 26. Science/ nature activities	**OTHER** Search Institute's 40 Developmental Assets #22/23 – children actively engaged in stimulating learning opportunities

	Standard	Grade/Age	Description
Benchmark or Learning Standard	Standards for Science (4th Ed.) Mid-continental Research for Education and Learning	Grade 3-5	Manipulation and Observation: understand that scientific explanations (observations) are based on experimentation and scientific knowledge Values and Attitudes: see that scientists share work with the public and other scientists and that they review other studies and ask questions about the results of other experiments Critical Response Skills: know that identical scientific experiments should result in similar if not the same evidence each time it is conducted
Benchmark or Learning Standard	Standards for Language Arts (4th Ed.) Mid-continental Research for Education and Learning	Grade 3	Use reading skills and strategies to comprehend instructions, texts, and passages
Benchmark or Learning Standard	Social Competence	All	Social Awareness: appreciating diversity Responsible Decision Making: respecting others, problem solving Relationship skills: communication, building relationships, negotiation
Benchmark or Learning Standard	National Content Standards for Physical Education	K-12	#6 – Demonstrates understanding and respect for differences among people in physical activity settings #7 – Understands that physical activity provides opportunities for enjoyment and social interaction

Section 6

Other Sample Science Activities

1. **"What Makes Paste?"** [30] (PreK-Grade 8) In this activity, children mix and match various harmless household ingredients such as baking soda, flour, cornstarch and salt along with water to determine which combination of ingredients makes a sticky paste. After testing the stickiness of each combination, they develop formulas that show how much of each ingredient works best.

2. **"River Cutters"** [31] (PreK-Grade 8) Children and youth create models of rivers in shallow plastic tubs filled with a special sand-like material and compare the structures that form in their model environment with creeks, rivers and lakes in their local areas. They design their own experiments in model bridge placement and block town building to test ideas about how water shapes the land.

3. **"Oobleck"** [32] (PreK-Grade 8) Oobleck (from Dr. Seuss's book *Bartholomew and the Oobleck*) is cornstarch mixed with just enough water that it will pour or dribble from your hand. Even though it pours like a liquid, it is also "hard" in that it will resist letting your finger sink into it. Oobleck can't be sculpted into a solid shape that lasts.

4. **"Height-O-Meters"** [33] Children and youth determine how tall or how high an object is by using an instrument called a clinometer made from diagrams in the GEMS guide and using techniques for converting the clinometer readings into feet, also described in the booklet. One task is to try to measure how high a tennis ball is thrown in the air.

5. **"Garbage Dump"** [34] Invites children and youth to learn about the techniques and science of separating one kind of material from another. The "garbage dump" activity challenges kids to figure out a way to separate a mixture of sand, salt, metal and wax without touching the mixture with their hands. Doing this successfully requires children to have participated in earlier experiences involving magnets, water, absorbent paper and sifters.

6. **"Paper Towel Testing"** [35] Children test the claims paper towel manufacturers make concerning the absorbency, strength and economy of their particular paper towel. For example: "How many metal washers can be piled on a damp sheet of towel before the towel rips?"; "How much water can one sheet of towel absorb before it is saturated and can't absorb any more water?"; or "How do rolls compare to each other in cost per sheet?"

7. **"Gliders"** [36] Children construct simple airplanes by folding and/or taping index cards. After testing a variety of wing and body designs, children are challenged to add tails to the glider to add stability. Towards the end of the study, rubber band launchers are developed to propel the launching of the glider, thereby adding flight distance that can be recorded and improved with each design variable change.

---

[30] Sample activity from GEMS Secret Formulas. (See Additional Science Resources.)
[31] Sample activity from GEMS River Cutters. (See Additional Science Resources.)
[32] Sample activity from GEMS Oobleck. (See Additional Science Resources.)
[33] Sample activity from GEMS Height-O-Meters. (See Additional Science Resources.)
[34] Sample activity from GEMS Sifting Through Science. (See Additional Science Resources.)
[35] Sample activity from GEMS Paper Towel Testing. (See Additional Science Resources.)
[36] Sample activity from Design-It! Gliders. (See Additional Science Resources.)

8. **"Trebuchets"** [37] A trebuchet is a catapult or sling shot that was used to toss objects high in the air or over far distances during wartime encounters in the Middle Ages. In the style of these early engineers, children use long yardsticks, heavy washers, rubber bands, filled plastic jugs and non-lethal objects like wads of paper wrapped with masking tape, to design a trebuchet which can launch a weight far distances, great heights, or hit targets with precision accuracy.

9. **"Balls and Tracks"** [38] Children using flexible foam pipe insulation, marbles and masking tape to design, create and test small-scale models of amusement park rides, ski jumps and games of skill. Applying just the right curve and shape to a foam track and finding just the right combination of chairs, tables and walls to hang the track on, children attempt to select the ideal pitch for getting a rolling marble into a cup on the floor. Or they can design the best "loop-the-loop" course.

Additional Science Resources

1. **Center for Science Education (CSE),** a project of the Education Development Center, Inc. has a website full of information on science education. EDC's award-winning programs and products build bridges between research, policy and practice. **http://cse.edc.org** Examples of CSE programs include:

   a. **The Center for Science Education @ Space Sciences Laboratory** Engaging web-based and hands-on science activities developed by educators and scientists in partnership with elementary-school teachers. Programs include coordination and support of NASA Sun-Earth Connection, education and outreach from satellite missions and programs, web-based curriculum and Eye on the Sky. **http://cse.ssl.berkeley.edu**

   b. **DESIGN-IT!: Engineering in After School Programs** is a nationally implemented and tested after-school curriculum project supported by science museums and centers. Activities help children develop basic engineering skills including trouble-shooting, design and re-design based on trials, testing, record keeping, problem solving and creativity. **http://cse.edc.org/work/designit/default.asp**

2. **Federal Resources for Educational Excellence (FREE) Science Resources** features a vast directory of resources in a variety of scientific fields, including astronomy, biology, earth science, ecology, geology and paleontology. **http://wdcrobcolp01.ed.gov/cfapps/free/displaysubject.cfm?sid=8**

3. **Frank Potter's Science Gems** is a website for students, parents, teachers, scientists, engineers, and mathematicians. The site includes links to more than 14,000 science resources sorted by category, sub-category and grade level. **www.sciencegems.com**

4. **Fun Science Resources Especially for Students** focuses on earth science and zoology, offering a variety of activities and research resources for grade school through middle-school age students. **www.reachoutmichigan.org/resources.html**

---

[37] Sample activity from Design-It! Trebuchets. (See Additional Science Resources.)
[38] Sample activity from Design It! Balls and Tracks. (See Additional Science Resources.)

Section 6

5. **GEMS - Great Explorations in Math and Science** curriculum guides (70+) offer varied science learning opportunities from PreK - 8th grade and can be presented by an adult without a background in science. The guides have been extensively tested and are aligned with the National Science Education Standards and are supplemented with the scientific principles and concepts that explain the science being experienced. The GEMS series includes more than 70 teacher's guides and handbooks for PreK - 8th grade, available from: LHS GEMS, Lawrence Hall of Science, University of California, Berkeley, CA 94720-5200. (510) 642-7771. **www.lhsgems.org**

6. **Math and Science Across Cultures** (ages 10-16) uses games and daily chore activities from many cultures to help learners understand other cultures, as well as the day-to-day importance of math and science for people of many societies. The activities use information-gathering tools to enable identifying patterns in data collected, interpreting data and applying logic to unravel compelling puzzles. **www.exploratoriumstore.edu** From Math and Science Across Cultures, published by The New Press, ©Exploratorium. **www.exploratorium.edu**

7. **National Aeronautics and Space Administration (NASA)** has for years developed curriculum activities and support materials for teachers interested in including space and aeronautics in their science curriculum, and is now extending to after-school programs. NASA offers educational articles, lesson plans, video tapes, CD's, DVD's, maps, photographs and colorful drawings of the solar system, launch and space vehicles, Earth Science and related topics, plus photos and sketches of Lunar Landers and Mars Surface Rovers. Materials can be found in the NASA Central Operation of Resources for Educators (CORE) catalog. **http://core.nasa.gov, http://education.nasa.gov, http://spacelink.nasa.gov/ercn**

8. **SciEd: Science and Mathematics Education Resources** is an extensive listing of educational science links in a variety of fields. It includes sections on science history, ethics in science, skepticism and pseudo-science and science education organizations. **http://newton.physics.wwu.edu:8082/jstewart/scied/science.html**

9. **The Science Center** is a chemistry-oriented site for younger learners. The Compound of the Month section features in-depth exploration of elemental and molecular structure. It also includes a science center bookstore. **www.science-education.org**

10. **Teacher-Student Science Resources** website focuses on astronomy and space technology. It offers resources for both teachers and students. **www.kidscosmos.org**

Math Problem Solving

For many people, math problem solving is associated with assigned homework for math class. For some, the association conjures up unpleasant memories. Negative associations with math often stem from mathematics instruction being separated from practical problem solving, instead being grounded in textbook exercises, isolated from other subjects and delivered in a teacher-centered context. After-school activities can create a bridge wherein newly learned math skills can be practiced in fun, practical, problem solving situations.

Why Include Math Problem Solving in After-School Programs?

Mathematical understanding for a child often begins with a real, personally meaningful problem that needs to be addressed in a mathematical way. Remember when you had to figure out if you could afford two candy bars with the money clutched in your sweaty palm? The use of pictures, tables, physical actions, diagrams and concrete "manipulatives" helps children develop math understanding and are easily incorporated into many after-school activities. These tools, and the "real child solutions" described below, aid in developing mathematical literacy. Knowing the concepts and procedures of math and using these ideas to solve problems that occur in a variety of situations constitutes "math literacy."

The following are problem-solving and mathematical skills that can be taught and reinforced in after-school activities:

- Recording Data (charting, graphing, tallying, etc.)
- Predicting
- Computing (adding, subtracting, multiplying, dividing)
- Measuring
- Determining Probability

Real Child Solutions [39]

One of the reasons problem solving has a troublesome reputation is the need to recall and use formulas and procedures that sometimes just don't make sense to the problem solver. *Real child solutions* are problem solving strategies that are instinctually used throughout the world, even among children and adults who have never been to school! Drawing, acting the problem out, or breaking the problem up into manageable parts are examples of *real child solutions*. Many *real child solutions* are useful in non-mathematical problem-solving experiences too, so learning and using them gives the learners insight into solving all kinds of personal, social and even physical problems encountered in life.

---

[39] From: National Center for Research in Mathematics Education and the Freudenthal Institute (Eds.) *Mathematics in context: A connected curriculum for grades 5-8*. Chicago: Encyclopedia Britannica Educational Corporation.

There are seven *real child solutions* or strategies used to solve problems that do not require algorithmic tools (mathematical formulas, multiplication or division). The seven strategies are:

1. **Look for a Pattern**

   Look for some kind of regularity to the problem data, which can lead to a rule or generalization. Patterns can occur in numbers, matrices and designs.

2. **Make a List**

   Words, numbers and units placed in a list are symbols that represent the real things being considered in the problem. Examples of lists: tallies, graphs, calendars and items to be checked off.

3. **Act it Out**

   Acting out the problem helps the problem solver model what might have been seen or what was actually described. While acting it out, people concretely experience the events embedded in the problem.

4. **Guess and Test, Try and See**

   Depend on initial thoughts, instincts and/or impulses in the absence of any other ideas or knowledge.

5. **Make a Model, Picture or Diagram**

   Make a literal or realistic image of the problem.

6. **Break into Parts**

   Reduce the problem into manageable units that can be considered one at a time.

7. **Work Backwards**

   Deconstruct the problem from back to front. This can happen when the answer to the problem is known. Take the problem apart, by starting with the answer and trying one thing after another in order to figure out where the answer must have come from.

Mathematics as a Descriptive Language

Mathematics can be thought of as a descriptive language that can be woven into many of the activities appropriate to after-school programming. Mathematical words, concepts and ways of thinking can be used to describe everyday things and their relationships to other things, (e.g. amount or number words, shape words, area words, geometry words, etc.) [40]

---

[40] See the "Mathematics: Concepts and Operations" chart which follows for more sources of math language.

Using Mathematics as a Descriptive Language

Task: Use the language of mathematics to describe and compare two leaves picked up from the ground.

The following is a typical, short response to this exercise. Even though this is a science observation experience – reminiscent of what might be heard on an after-school program walk through the park – as you read it, you can identify many mathematics words and concepts.

"One oval-shaped leaf is bigger than the other oval-shaped leaf. The larger one is about twice the area of the smaller one. There are 10 veins on each side of the central vein in the small leaf, meaning 20 veins all together on the smaller leaf, and 14 veins on each side of the central vein of the larger one, meaning 28 veins altogether on the larger leaf. Each vein ends at a wedge-shaped point at the edge of the leaf, as in a saw's tooth. The veins on each side of the central vein do not, however, emerge at the same point. The veins emerging to the right side of the leaf, when looked at from its "sun side" surface, emerge slightly above the veins emerging to the left side. The leaves are both light brown in color, each with a few darker brown spots located randomly across the surface of the leaf."

Mathematics: Concepts and Operations

The following three lists provide ways to think about how different math concepts cluster and become sources of the math language that can describe things. Thinking about these three concepts – relationships, calculations and operations – gives you another context for incorporating math problem solving into your program activities.

I. The Language of Mathematical Relationships
Presented in relational order from basic to complex.

- One-to-One Correspondence: object-to-object correspondence by some (non-mathematical) criteria
- Equivalence: object-to-object correspondence by some mathematical criteria
- Classification/Grouping with labels: objects grouped by some commonly held criteria
- Sequence: an ordered arrangement of some sort (as in steps in a recipe, dance, schedule)
- Series: an ordered arrangement of objects informed by an incremental change in the quantity or quality of one of that object's attributes
- Value without number assigned: big, small, lots, tiny, etc.
- Value with number assigned: Number sense
- Cardinal Numbers: 1,2,3,4,5 (counting)
- Ordinal Numbers: first, second, third, etc. (order)
- Patterns: a numeric or geometric logically organized arrangement.
- Part/Whole relationships: percentages, fractions, ratios
- Estimations
- Tessellations: logically arranged geometric shapes creating a whole, continuous pattern, e.g. checkered or mosaic
- Geometry and Spatial Sense: shapes and forms (Euclidean and Abstract)
- Symmetry

II. The Language of Calculable Relationships

- Relationships and Ratios
- Lengths
- Widths
- Depths
- Shapes
- Areas
- Weights
- Speeds
- Volumes
- Time
- Lines, curves
- Angles

III. The Language of Mathematical Concepts/Skills Linked to Operations

- Recording Data (charting, graphing, tallying)
- Problem Solving, Algebra
- Prediction
- Computing (add, subtract, multiply, divide)
- Measuring
- Determining Probability
- Algebra and Statistics

Occasions for Problem Solving and Using Math Language

- **Daily Problem**: Each day, a new problem is posted at the entrance to the program site. Children put their solutions in a box to be considered at the end of the day.

- **Problem-Solving Club**: A regular weekly meeting time when interested youth gather to solve interesting math problems. This might be the occasion when the leaders can introduce children to tools that help in solving problems – such as rulers, yard sticks, tape measures, levels, calculators and compasses. In some programs, Problem-Solving Clubs gather to discuss and suggest solutions not only to math problems but also to real social, behavioral and other program problems inherent in the program.

- **Transition**: As a transition activity between one program experience and another, e.g. while children and youth are lined up but needing to wait for buses, parents, or the next experience on the schedule.

- **Integrated into other activities**: Use the language of mathematics when:
  - Observing objects and occurrences while on field trips or during science explorations.
  - Telling stories about recent experiences to others.
  - Writing articles for the program's newspaper.
  - Describing in words or developing maps about how to get from one place to another.

Math for Transitions

In an after-school program where children rehearsed and performed in a local *Nutcracker* ballet performance, a staff person got children excited about math problem solving by doing problems with them while they were waiting to either rehearse or perform. Instead of letting them become bored or aggressive, he filled their idle time by engaging children of all ages and math abilities in the fun of solving problems. While they waited in line, he would throw out a problem for them to consider. Children who had ideas about the solution expressed them. Others soon followed suit. The secret to his success was giving them hints or clues – as well as problems they could personally relate to and picture in their minds – and opening up the problem solving process by using *real child solutions*.

Sample Math Problem Solving Activity Plan

Title

Cookie/Sneaker/Paper Snowflake/Valentine* Factory

Description

Solve all the math problems related to launching a "real-world" business including: design of product, design and construction of facility, calculations for materials, purchase of supplies, price of goods, pay for workers, etc.

Objectives

Provide "real world" problem-solving opportunities for children to practice math, social competence and literacy skills.

Intended Outcomes

- Children will gain experience solving math (and science) problems using number relationships, computation and estimation, measurement and communication skills.
- Children will gain experience working with others to solve problems and expand understanding.
- Children will gain experience and practice reading, writing, speaking and listening.

Special Materials and Tools

Calculators, raw materials for product "prototype."

Space Requirements

Space for discussions, progress reports. Table space for calculations and design work. Bulletin board or other display area for project conclusions.

Age/Group Size

Appropriate for children with at least 4th grade math skills.

The Activity

Brainstorm the "product" the group would like their factory to produce. Think of all the different number/measurement-related questions that will need to be answered. Put the tasks on a timeline and divide the group up to tackle the different questions.

Incorporating Technology

- Search the Internet for recipes, design ideas, etc.
- Use animation techniques to demonstrate factory production.
- For older children, incorporate use of computer-assisted design software for product or facility design.

Extensions and Continuations

Arrange a visit to a nearby factory. If the imagined factory is a food-related one, the activity could provide opportunities to gain nutritional or scientific knowledge.

Conclusions/Reflections

Compare estimates to actual calculations. Ask children to reflect on what their experience has taught them about the value of various goods.

Once the answers to the various numerical questions are found, create a display that shows how they were researched and calculated.

* The item that children wish to "produce" in the factory could be almost anything. Depending on what they choose, it could relate to nutrition, science, music, etc.

Section 6

Linking to Quality Standards and Learning Benchmarks

Activity Title	Cookie/Sneaker/Snowflake/Valentine Factory						
Description	Solve all the math-related problems related to launching a "real-world" business including: design of product, design and construction of facility calculations for materials, purchase of supplies, price of goods, pay for workers, etc.						

Core Content Area (check all that apply)	Math	Literacy	Science	Arts	Fitness/ Nutrition	Social Competence	Other
	✓	✓	✓		✓	✓	

Skills for the New Economy (check all that apply)	Numeracy	Communication		Problem solving	Technology		Work w/others
	✓	✓		✓	✓		✓

Quality Standards	NAA	SACERS	OTHER
	#4 – Staff interact with children to help them learn #13 – Activities reflect the mission of the program and promote the development of all children #28 – Staff and children work together to plan suitable activities	22. Blocks and construction 25. Math/ reasoning activities	Search Institute's 40 Developmental Assets #22/23 – children actively engaged in stimulating learning opportunities

	Standard	Grade/Age	Description
Benchmark or Learning Standard	Standards for Science (4th Ed.) Mid-continental Research for Education and Learning	Grade 4-8	<u>Math as Problem-Solving</u>: Use a variety of strategies to comprehend problem situations <u>Mathematical Connection</u>: Understand that mathematics can be helpful in other fields of study and has been used in other fields for centuries <u>Measurement</u>: grasp the basic measures of length, width, height, weight and temperature
Benchmark or Learning Standard	Standards for Language Arts (4th Ed.) Mid-continental Research for Education and Learning	Grade 4-8	<u>Reading</u>: Make connections between characters and events in text with people or events in own life <u>Writing</u>: Write to address problems, respond to literature, express ideas, and evaluate
Benchmark or Learning Standard	Social Competence	All	<u>Self-management</u>: Goal setting <u>Relationship skills</u>: communication, building relationships, negotiation
Benchmark or Learning Standard	Nutrition (if food-related)	All	Gain a better understanding of basic nutritional requirements Understand food safety issues and behaviors

Other Sample Math Problem Solving Activities

1. **"Sneeze Builds a Castle"** [41] (PreK-K) Develop spatial sense through building a castle with blocks.

2. **"Funny Bug"** [42] (Ages 5-8) Leader finds and reads a story featuring bugs (i.e., Eric Carle, *The Grouchy Ladybug*). Players agree on the number of rounds they want to play. Then they can create a "funny bug" by throwing two dice. The two numbers thrown by the first player are added together. Numbers are assigned to the bug body part to be drawn by that player at his/her turn. (e.g. #2 is a bug nose, #12 is a wing, #7 is a head and so forth.) Play continues until a bug with all its body parts is completed. The leader asks children to examine the drawing to answer individual math questions. "How many eyes does your bug have?" "Are there more wings than legs?" "Point to a circle shape in your drawing."

3. **"Greeting Card Boxes"** [43] (Grades 6-8) Children use old greeting cards, rulers, scissors, tape and calculators to make small storage boxes with lids. Before making the boxes from greeting cards, they practice making boxes from grid paper. Following directions and measurement skills are learned, refined and practiced while doing this activity. In the process, they learn about area and volume, important concepts in middle school geometry.

4. **"Tea and Temperature - Chinese Traditions"** [44] (Ages 10-16) Children study a traditionally prepared cup of Chinese tea to learn about heat energy flow away from the tea, through the porcelain cup and into the air around it. After learning about how the first cup of tea may have originated and spread as a culinary custom in China, learners use a thermometer to chart temperatures and changes to temperatures as a cup of tea cools down. Once this is understood, learners study the differences in cooling rates between cups with lids and ones without lids.

---

[41] Sample activity from *Round the Rug Math: Adventures in Problem Solving* (see Additional Math Resources).

[42] Sample activity from *Afterschool KidzMath*™ (see Additional Math Resources). Adapted from *Funny Bug*, authorized by Development Studies Center, 2002©, Oakland, CA 94606, (800) 666-7270, www.devstu.org.

[43] Sample activity from *Math Explorer* (see Additional Math Resources).

[44] Sample activity from *Math and Science Across Cultures* (see Additional Math Resources).

Section 6

Additional Math Problem Solving Resources

1. **Afterschool KidzMath™** (Grades 3-6) uses games and read-aloud activities after the reading of 10 different stories with math themes. Math concepts include number relationships, measurement and geometry. All activities have a social skill development component built into them. **www.kidzafterschool.org**

2. **Math Explorer** (Ages 10-16) offers hands-on math activities for middle-school youth to think about and approach math through puzzles, tricks and games, to apply math to specific experimentation and to use math in making and designing interesting things. The activities are engaging, creative and don't at all feel like schoolwork, yet they address state and national math learning standards for the middle school grades. Each activity plan includes: preparation materials, a planning chart, suggestions and steps for implementing the activity, templates and descriptions to help the instructor understand where the math and science content is highlighted during the activity. **www.exploratoriumstore.edu**. Also available from **www.AfterSchoolCatalog.com**

3. **Math and Science Across Cultures** (Grades 3-6) uses amusement games and daily chore activities from many cultures to help learners understand other cultures, as well as the day-to-day importance of math and science for people of many societies. The activities use information-gathering tools to enable identifying patterns in data collected, interpreting data and applying logic to unravel compelling puzzles. **www.exploratoriumstore.edu**

4. **MindWare: Brainy Toys for Kids of All Ages** A catalog of toys, manipulatives and activity guides written to challenge and build problem-solving skills. **www.MINDWAREonline.com**

5. **Round the Rug Math: Adventures in Problem Solving** (PreK-Grade 2) uses storytelling to introduce and teach mathematics. The character development, plot, suspense and resolution dimensions of good stories are used to help children develop estimation skills, measurement and spatial reasoning skills. Pictures, manipulatives, words and construction materials are the media used to engage children in the problem-solving tasks. These National Science Foundation funded program materials meet the National Council of Teachers of Mathematics (NCTM) standards. **www.Wrightgroup.com/cgi-bin/catalog/series.cgi**

Recommended Reading

1. Coates, G.C. and J.K. Stenmark, *Family Math for Young Children*. Chicago: Zephyr Press. 1997 (1-800-232-2187)

2. Stenmark, J.K., V. Thompson and R. Cossey, *Family Math*. Chicago: Zephyr Press. 1986

3. Thompson, V. and K.Mayfield-Ingram, *Family Math: The Middle School Years*. (1998). Chicago: Zephyr Press. 1998

4. National Center for Research in Mathematics Education and the Freudenthal Institute (Eds.) *"Mathematics in context: A connected curriculum for grades 5-8"*. Chicago: Encyclopedia Britannica Educational Corporation. http://mic.britannica.com/mic/common/home.asp

5. Zaslavsky, Claudia, *Math Games & Activities from Around the World*. Chicago: Chicago Review Press. 1998

Section 6

Arts Curriculum

Children are engaged in art when they:

- Participate in hands-on experiences with the tools and mediums of each art form (painting, drawing, sculpting, photography, collage, making ceramics, designing, dancing, music, theater, poetry, architecture and visual arts).

- Attend, observe and discuss exhibits, performances, galleries and museum collections.

- Establish and use a personal sense of what is and is not beautiful (an aesthetic).

- Critically evaluate and analyze the art they make and study.

- Begin to understand how all the arts relate to each other, as well as to other disciplines such as language, math, and science.

Why Include Arts in After-School Programs?

Research[45] has shown that children and youth who participate regularly in the arts:

- Show more creativity and originality in their thinking.
- Receive constructive criticism better.
- Ask more "what if" questions.
- Talk more freely about what they think and believe.
- Are more descriptive in their language.
- Have enhanced spatial reasoning skills.
- Are better at problem solving.
- Have more self-esteem, self-discipline and motivation.
- Allow and encourage more freedom of expression for themselves and others.

What Can Children and Youth Learn from Art?

- The tools, materials and techniques of each art form.
- The artistic languages for communicating ideas.
- That art reflects the history, symbols, myths, beliefs, and values of the cultures and personalities that created it.
- To validate and deepen their originality, imagination, and creative abilities.
- Discipline (the value of sustained effort) and the concrete rewards of hard work.
- The core competencies of thinking creatively, problem solving, exercising individual responsibility, sociability, and self-esteem.
- Potential career options in the arts.

---

[45] Heath, Shirley Brice and Adelma Aurora Roach. "The Arts in the Non-School Hours."
Carnegie Foundation for the Advancement of Teaching, March, 1998.

Environment

Great art happens in less than ideal environments, but there are some basic space requirements for each art form:

- The visual, sculptural, ceramic, and photographic arts are messy. Visual arts activities often need large tables, natural light, easels, sinks and places for storing art supplies and partly finished art works. Potters need pottery studios with large flat tables, potter's wheels, material and project storage, sinks and kiln space. The spaces used for these potentially messy art forms must be easily cleaned.

- Poets need writing areas and environments that inspire ideas.

- All art forms, even dance and theater, need places to store raw materials (props, production tools and lighting materials) safely.

- Drama needs space for the actors and the audience. Dance requires the same and a "sprung floor" (wooden flooring that gives a little when it's jumped on) is preferable.

- All art forms eventually create products (plays, dances, paintings, ceramic pieces, photographs or poems) that should be performed, archived or displayed for others to see. Performance and display spaces are important for sustaining interest in the arts for all ages.

Daily Schedule

Children and youth vary in their commitment to various art forms. Ideally, art areas should be open every day. Children and youth who like to dabble in the various arts materials and techniques can drop in once in a while. Those who want to do art every day can come for prolonged periods. This makes it possible for the child who really wants to explore an idea in depth to do so. In any case, there should be a knowledgeable adult leader assigned to all arts areas to help the children.

Some programs use an "Art Club" to enable the seriously interested child to explore an art in depth. Clubs can offer a wide array of experiences associated with a particular art or craft form. For example a "Pottery Club" can offer opportunities for children and youth to make ceramic objects, visit professional ceramists at work in their studios, attend gallery shows of ceramic objects, interview a famous artist, or organize a sale of clay objects made at the program site.

Age and Development

Some of education's most contentious debates can be found in discussions of how to provide learning experiences in the arts. The issue most often debated concerns whether or not to teach art technique to children. Some feel that children should "mess about" developing and discovering artistic techniques on their own. Others believe in teaching art techniques such as shading or perspective, then allowing lots of time for children to practice these techniques. Patterned art such as the kind of activity where everybody's pre-cut rabbit needs a cotton ball glued on to make the rabbit's tail makes some people applaud while others go into rages about the lack of individuality inherent in this activity. Some say that classical ballet is at the heart of every dance form, while others are convinced that classical ballet training stunts the creativity that can often be observed in modern dance forms. Poetry with rhyming lines is better, some say, than non-rhyming verse. Memorizing play lines is better theater training, some argue, than reading the play. Pottery is not an art but a craft, say some. Photography isn't art or craft but technology.

Perhaps the first thing you need to do is to sort through and determine where you stand on some of these issues before you think about selecting activities. In the field of art education you will always find a population that agrees with your stand and one which doesn't.

In general, every art form requires an initial period for the learner to become familiar with the tools, materials, mediums and techniques associated with it. During this period, the artist learns about the properties of the tools and materials, learning what each can and cannot do. This process can be formal and focused or have a lot of messing-about associated with it. However, once the properties and potentials of the media, tools and techniques are understood, leaders can suggest organized and intentional art activities to challenge children's understanding and enlarge their opportunities to learn.

Sample Arts Activity Plan

Title

Many Arts

Description

Use arts as a language through which children and youth can express understanding of a particular topic or concept.

Objectives

Provide opportunity for children and youth to explore and experience different art forms while simultaneously gaining literacy and social-competence skills and exploring a topic of interest to them.

Intended Outcomes

- Children and youth will gain experience and practice with different artistic media and learn how to express new knowledge or understanding using these tools.
- Children and youth will gain experience and practice reading, writing, speaking and listening.
- Children and youth will learn to work with and learn from others.

Special Materials and Tools

Appropriate artistic materials (e.g. paint, clay, musical instruments, etc.)

Space Requirements

Room to comfortably gather for discussions, tables to work at/write on, storage for ongoing art project materials, stage or performing space, bulletin boards.

Age/Group Size

Appropriate for ages 10-18. This project could involve many children and youth or just a few depending on the available guest artists.

The Activity

Youth identify and research a selected topic or concept by reading about it, listening to presentations, visiting museums or galleries that feature the concept, and/or holding discussions about it (e.g. "Waste not, Want not," "Risk & Chance," "Time," "Living on the Edge," "New Millenium"). After gaining a thorough understanding of the topic, children and youth apprentice with different locally available artists who set up their studios in the after-school program (e.g. painter, sculptor, dancer, poet, weaver, dramatist, photographer, potter). Each child chooses three artists whose art forms they are curious about, or whose art media and techniques they think are most appropriate for the concept they wish to represent. Youth will be asked to represent their own particular understanding of the chosen concept in one of the art forms for a final exhibition.

Section 6

Incorporating Technology

- Make web design one of the possible art forms to apprentice.
- Use Internet to research selected topic and/or art form.
- Create website/web pages for permanent display of children and youth's work.

Extensions and Continuations

Children and youth can choose more than one art form to represent their ideas or can research more than one concept. Children and youth can form groups to work together to represent their ideas, especially in the performing arts.

Conclusions/Reflections

Have children and youth present their work to the group, allowing opportunities for questions and answers among the learners.

Documentation

Hold an exhibition of what each youth considers his or her best representation of the topic/concept. The exhibition will be for family and friends and could be judged by a panel of adults or peers.

Linking to Quality Standards and Learning Benchmarks

Activity Title	**Many Arts**						
Description	Use arts as a language through which children and youth can express understanding of a particular topic or concept.						

Core Content Area (check all that apply)	Math	Literacy	Science	Arts	Fitness/ Nutrition	Social Competence	Other
		✓		✓		✓	

Skills for the New Economy (check all that apply)	Numeracy	Communication		Problem solving	Technology	Work w/others
		✓		✓	✓	✓

Quality Standards	**NAA** #13 – Children can choose from a variety of activities #15 – There are sufficient materials to support program activities #25 – The program builds links to the community	**SACERS** 20. Arts and crafts 21. Music and movement 23. Drama and theatre	**OTHER** Search Institute's 40 Developmental Assets #7 - children feel the community values and appreciate them #22/23 - children actively engaged in stimulating learning opportunities

	Standard	**Grade/Age**	**Description**
Benchmark or Learning Standard	ArtsEdge National Standard for Arts Education	All	<u>Production and Performance</u>: understand art as a venue for communicating ideas and meanings, connect and compare various art forms <u>Imaginative, Critical and Reflective Thinking</u>: analyze and explain personal artistic preferences, construct meaning from art <u>Understanding cultural and historical contexts</u>: demonstrate and understand the use of art in various cultures and throughout history
Benchmark or Learning Standard	Social Competence	All	<u>Self-awareness</u>: recognizing strengths <u>Social-awareness</u>: perspective taking <u>Self-management</u>: goal setting <u>Relationship skills</u>: communication, building relationships, negotiation
Benchmark or Learning Standard	Standards for Language Arts (4th Ed.) Mid-continent Research for Education and Learning	Grade 3 Grade 6	▪ Establish purpose for reading (e.g. fun, information, understand varying points of view) ▪ Use a variety of strategies to create writing (e.g. draft outline, brainstorms, topic research) ▪ Make connections between characters and events in own life

Section 6

Other Sample Arts Activities

1. **"Water Painting"**[46] Use water to 'paint' objects with a bright, shiny coat of water or paint designs on paper or pavement. Watch as the designs evaporate, or disappear. Try to describe what you see and why as this occurs.

2. **"Saw Dust Mixture"**[47] Make a modeling material that has a wood-like quality using sawdust and wallpaper paste. Squeeze and pat the modeling mixture into a desired shape. Paint with tempura paint when dry, if desired.

3. **"Nature Paintbrush"**[48] Test and experiment with the visual effects different twigs, flowers, feathers and ferns have when dipped in paint and used as paint brushes. Adult can demonstrate how to hold, dip and experimentally apply paint to create different effects on paper.

4. **"On-Site Beach Art"**[49] Use natural and commonly occurring "found" beach (or forest, field, mountain top and desert) materials to make designs, collages, structures, or pictures which, once completed, are left to change in the natural elements of out-of-doors.

5. **"Linking To Cultural Institutions"** Introduce children and youth to local museums, dance and theater companies, orchestras, science centers and other places where they might begin to recognize new interests and abilities. Provide them with an inside look behind the scenes at these institutions: back stage at the theater company, job shadowing an artist, sitting in the orchestra pit, etc. Note the things each child seems to be most interested in and develop special after-school activities, "fanning the sparks" of a child's particular kind or blend of intelligence.

6. **"Artworks Exchange: A Celebration of Our Culture's Universals"**
A "pen-pals" program-to-program exchange of artwork meant to convey information about the young artists and what is important to them. Each group is asked to depict things that they know the other artists live with too. For example, depict the sun, moon and stars, but place them in settings that reveal the houses, foods, plants, people and communities in which each artist lives. Or represent *applause, anger, an argument, happy, dreaming, not thinking, animals sleeping, hungry.* Celebrate and applaud the diversity of ways all the children or youth depict or "see" a concept.

---

[46] Sample activity from: *Science Arts: Discovering Science Through Art Experiences.* Bellingham, WA: Bright Ring Publishing. 1993. (See additional Art Resources.)

[47] Sample activity from: *Mudworks: Creative Clay, Dough, and Modeling Experiences.* Bellingham, WA: Bright Ring Publishing. 1989. (See additional Art Resources.)

[48-49] Sample activity from: *Good Earth Art: Environmental Art for Kids.* Bellingham, WA: Bright Ring Publishing. 1991. (See additional Art Resources.)

7. **"Portrait of a Statue"** Students visit, photograph, draw, measure, touch, explore, interview, "get to know" a nearby statue then make a portrait – drawing, sculpture, model, or theatrical representation – of the statue they visited. Paint, clay, markers, pencils, paper, tools for measuring, cameras for picture taking, aluminum foil for making impressions if possible should be made available during both parts of this experience.

8. **"Spicy Paints Study"** Study how common spice powders (turmeric, clove, mustard powder, parsley, cinnamon, thyme, saffron) alone or blended with other spices and mixed with glue make colored paints. Develop a paint-making recipe book of the group's favorite colors and how to make them. Try variations called "Berry Spicy Paints" or "Flower Spicy Paints" using berries or flower petals mixed with the spices to create other colors.

Additional Arts Resources

1. **Americans for the Arts** has produced the **YouthARTS** website and tool kit designed to give arts agencies, juvenile justice agencies, social service organizations and other community-based organizations detailed information about how to plan, run, provide training and evaluate arts programs for at-risk youth. Based on rigorous research, the kit features a step-by-step handbook, sample forms and other materials already in use by youth arts programs. **www.artsusa.org/youtharts**

2. **ARTSEDGE, the National Arts and Education Network** empowers educators to teach in, through and about the arts by providing the tools to develop interdisciplinary curricula that fully integrate the arts with other academic subjects. ARTSEDGE offers free, standards-based lesson plans for use in and out of the classroom, as well as professional development resources, student materials and guidelines for arts-based instruction and assessment. **www.artsedge.kennedy-center.org**

3. **The Arts Education Partnership** is a national coalition of arts, education, business, philanthropic and government organizations that demonstrates and promotes the essential role of the arts in the learning and development of every child and in the improvement of America's schools. **www.aep-arts.org**

4. **Bright Ideas for Learning** is a series of art activity booklets that use commonly available, safe and inexpensive materials and tools. The activities are often open-ended and encourage the artistic process more than the creation of products. Each activity is coded to help the leader identify activities that are appropriate for specific needs of children, adults, the season, etc. The activities also connect to other key learning areas like math and science. Some of the titles in this series: *Science Arts: Discovering Science Through Art Experiences; Good Earth Art: Environmental Art for Kids; Cooking Art: Easy Edible Art for Young Children; Make Make-Believe: Fun Props, Costumes and Creative Play Ideas; Pre-school Art: It's the Process, Not the Product.* **www.brightring.com**

5. **How the Arts Can Enhance After-School Programs** is a website sponsored by the U.S. Department of Education and the National Endowment for the Arts. The website offers a variety of resources – articles, techniques, federal partnerships and resource directories. **www.arts.gov/pub/ArtsAfter-school/artsedpub.html**

6. **School-Age Notes** is a resource organization that develops and provides information, technical assistance and resources concerning children and youth in out-of-school settings. In their online catalog they have numerous art activity books. **www.AfterSchoolCatalog.com**

Recommended Reading

1. Murfee, Elizabeth. *Eloquent Evidence: Arts at the Core of Learning.* A publication of the President's Committee on the Arts and the Humanities and the National Assembly of State Arts Agencies. Washington, D.C.: National Endowment for the Arts. October, 1995. www.nasaa-arts.org/nasaanews/ee.pdf

2. *Schools, Communities, and the Arts: A Research Compendium.* Washington, D.C.: Kennedy Center Alliance for Arts Education Network. 1996. Available as a PDF: www.asu.edu/copp/morrison/public/schools.pdf

3. Charlip, Remy & The San Francisco Arts Education Project. *Ideas for Teaching the Arts to Children.* San Francisco: Threshold Foundation. 1995. www.remycharlip.com/books.html

Social Competence

There is growing evidence that attending to the social and emotional development of children and youth is an important key to their academic success. Indeed, Daniel Goleman, the author of *Emotional Intelligence* – a book that popularized much of the research on social/emotional learning – asserts that as much as 80 percent of a person's success rests on his or her emotional intelligence.[50] Furthermore, unlike IQ, which many believe you are essentially born with, emotional intelligence is something you can learn and develop over time. After-school programs are especially well suited to nurture emotional and social development for many reasons, including the fact that relationships between adults and children are less formal and task-driven than they are in a typical school setting.

To succeed, after-school programs must be places where children, youth and adults feel safe, understood, respected and secure.[51] When these basic requirements for healthy living and socializing are missing, learning rarely takes place. Social competence and conflict resolution activities – when incorporated into ongoing, daily programming – help make programs emotionally and socially comfortable places to be. These activities provide children and youth with strategies for dealing with conflict when it comes their way and help them develop socially acceptable ways of interacting with one another.

---

[50] Goleman, Daniel. *Emotional Intelligence: Why it can matter more than IQ.* New York: Bantam Books. 1997.

[51] Seligson, Michelle and Patricia Stahl, *Bringing Yourself to Work: A Guide to Successful Staff Development in After-School Programs.* Teachers College Press. 2003.

Why Include Social-Competence Activities in After-School Programs?

Getting along with others, living and playing by the rules, developing friendships and being a friend, respecting and helping others are things we all must learn in the every-day context of being with other people. These are but a few of the behaviors that make it possible for people to work together, pool energies and talents and complete jobs more effectively than we could have on our own. The lessons of social competence come hour by hour, day by day, in everything we do.

Conflict is a part of everyone's life. Conflicts arise because people think about things in very different ways. When conflict is destructive, it may be because the individuals do not recognize that there are several reasonable ways, not just one way, to think about something. Programs that are characterized by people who know how to get along with others emphasize five general themes:

- Cooperation
- Communication
- Expression of feelings
- Valuing diversity
- Peaceful conflict resolution

"Adventure learning" is a term used to describe personal-growth experiences in which people are required to work together to test and develop problem-solving skills, motivation, creativity, cooperation, an appreciation of diversity, conflict-resolution skills and leadership, usually in the context of an outdoor or physically-challenging activity. Adventure-learning activities are another way after-school programs can help children and youth develop social and emotional competence.

What Can Children and Youth Learn from Social-Competence Activities?

- Self confidence, self awareness and self control
- Leadership skills
- How to peacefully resolve conflicts
- An appreciation of diversity among people
- Creative problem-solving skills
- A realistic sense of self
- To listen to, trust and respect others
- To take constructive personal risks and to learn from these
- To work effectively in groups on challenging tasks

Environment

The nature of many social-competence and conflict-resolution experiences involves children and youth being honest and taking risks with their thoughts and emotions. Risk taking of this type should be done in an environment that includes other people who understand and support it rather than in a public arena where the potential is real for "outsiders" to laugh at or mock what is going on. Activities of this nature are facilitated by collectively created ground rules for acceptable behavior. Developed by both children and staff, posted on the wall, consistently and regularly reinforced and revised when necessary, these rules help all understand the acceptable and agreed upon behavioral boundaries.

In their book *Adventures in Peacemaking*, Educators for Social Responsibility (ESR), one of the leading groups specializing in conflict-resolution and social-competence curriculum and activity development, suggest setting up a "Peace Place" for children and youth to use in resolving conflicts. All children are introduced to the Peace Place, told what it is used for and given a demonstration of how to use it. Whenever a conflict arises, children are asked to go to the Peace Place, where they are given seven minutes to come up with a resolution on their own before an adult will intervene to help. For middle-school age youth, ESR refers to the conflict-resolution environment not as a physical place, but as an emotional place where children and youth feel safe as they engage in activities and discussions that build their social competence.

Daily Schedule

Teaching social competence is an ongoing effort, though some programs regularly schedule activities and experiences meant to help children and youth develop the skills to get along better on a regular basis. Wise adults help children and youth develop these skills by having established, <u>before the need arises</u>, predictable and consistent schedules, leadership, rules and expectations that make for socially and emotionally safe places. These basics tend to minimize, but can not eliminate, the potential for conflict and socially unacceptable behaviors. Building social and emotional competence through regularly scheduled activities can also reduce the likelihood or frequency of undesirable behaviors.

Social Competence of Caregivers

In addition to attending to the social and emotional needs and development of children and youth, there is a growing body of research on the importance of emotional intelligence among after-school staff and the need for training and support in these areas. **Bringing Yourself to Work**, an organization devoted to supporting after-school caregivers, has collected significant research on this topic.

Among the most important findings: [52]

- Programs emphasizing the personal development of adult educators have a more positive social-emotional climate than those that do not address adult development issues.

- Successful after-school programs build in opportunities for staff to reflect on what leads them to work with children and youth and how these motivations affect their relationships with children and youth.

- Providing emotional and relational skill-building training for after-school providers offers them essential coping tools in an undervalued profession.

Age and Development

According to ESR, the best activities in social development and conflict resolution for young children (ages 6-10) have the following characteristics:

- They help children recognize there are varied ways of thinking about something.
- They use discussion to look at problems from varied perspectives.
- They help children understand that a particular situation can be good and bad and some place in the middle all at once.
- They acquaint children with how issues are linked to other less apparent issues and may help explain events.
- They let children know that they have a job to do in making a situation better and that change is possible.

According to ESR, middle-school youth (ages 11-16) profit when social development and conflict resolution activities:

- Provide opportunities for positive social interaction, sometimes referred to as community-building activities, and reduce exclusionary behaviors.
- Help youth explore their identities on their own or in small groups, where they will be exposed to others' points of view.
- Model skillful behavior around conflict.
- Provide opportunities for practicing conflict resolution.
- Build autonomy.
- Give both children and youth safe places to voice their feelings.
- Have clear limits and expectations.
- Provide varied opportunities to explore competence and achievement.

---

[52] Seligson, Michelle and Patricia Stahl, *Bringing Yourself to Work: A Guide to Successful Staff Development in After-School Programs*, Teachers College Press. 2003.

Sample Social-Competence Activity Plan

Title

Photo Voices Project

Description

Invite children and youth to take photographs of "important," "need to change" and "perfect" things about their neighborhood/community. Discuss and record their feelings and understandings and display the artwork for the larger community.

Objectives

Use photography as a medium for children and youth to learn about and express their understandings of their world, neighborhood or school/program, and to appreciate the perspectives of others.

Intended Outcomes

- Children and youth will build social awareness and gain skills in self-expression and self-awareness.
- Children and youth will gain perspective on self and an appreciation of diversity.
- Children and youth will gain skills in photography, writing, speaking and listening.

Special Materials and Tools

Cameras, film, developing capacity (or computer and printer if digital cameras), writing materials, mounting/display materials.

Space Requirements

Discussion area, display area, storage for ongoing project.

Age/Group Size

Could involve a few children or large group. Best suited to older children, ages 10-14.

The Activity

Invite children to take photographs of the physical and social things in a community they think are:

    a. Very important

    b. Need to be changed

    c. Perfect just as they are

1. Solicit, record and display the ideas/feelings each photographer generated as s/he discussed the individual photographs.
2. Invite parents, community members and others to visit the photo display and interpretation.

Incorporating Technology

- Using digital cameras and computer imaging software.
- Create Powerpoint presentation of children's conclusions about their community.

Extensions and Continuations

- Invite local elected officials to display and discussion of children and youth's conclusions.
- Use other art media – paintings, murals, drawings, etc. for similar project.
- Select something that "needs to be changed" for local community service project.
- Host art show opening and invite local media to see and hear youth's views.

Section 6

Conclusions/Reflections

Discuss children and youth's understandings of the potential of this medium to communicate ideas, feelings or thoughts for social/personal change.

Documentation

Record number of photos taken and content or associated dialogue for each child.

Linking to Quality Standards and Learning Benchmarks

Activity Title	Photo Voices Project						
Description	Invite children and youth to take photographs of "important," "need to change" and "perfect" things about their neighborhood/community. Discuss and record their feelings and understandings and display artwork for the larger community.						

Core Content Area (check all that apply)	Math	Literacy	Science	Arts	Fitness/ Nutrition	Social Competence	Other
		✓		✓		✓	

Skills for the New Economy (check all that apply)	Numeracy	Communication		Problem solving	Technology	Work w/others
		✓			✓	✓

Quality Standards	NAA	SACERS	OTHER
	#4 – Staff interact with children to help them learn #14 – Activities reflect the mission and promote the development of the children #25 – The program builds links to the community	20. Arts and crafts 27. Cultural awareness 40. Use of community resources	Search Institute's 40 Developmental Assets #27 - Equality and Social Justice: children show interest in making the community a better place

	Standard	Grade/Age	Description
Benchmark or Learning Standard	CASEL Social Emotional Learning Competencies	N/A	<u>Self-awareness</u>: identifying emotions and recognizing strengths <u>Social-awareness</u>: perspective taking and appreciating diversity <u>Relationship skills</u>: communication, building relationships
Benchmark or Learning Standard	ArtsEdge National Standards for Arts Education	N/A	<u>Production and Performance</u>: understand art as a venue for communicating ideas and meanings, connect and compare various art forms <u>Imaginative, Critical and Reflective Thinking</u>: apply and demonstrate critical thinking skills in art, analyze and evaluate others' artwork <u>Understanding Cultural and Historical Contexts</u>: share knowledge about the use of art in various cultures and throughout history
Benchmark or Learning Standard	Standards for Language Arts (4th Ed.) Mid-continent Research for Education and Learning	Ages 11-12	<u>Reading</u>: make connections between characters and events in text with people or events in own life <u>Writing</u>: use pre-writing strategies to organize written work, use correct grammatical rules in writing, and write to address problems, respond to literature, express ideas, and evaluate

Section 6

Other Sample Social-Competence Activities

1. **"Concentration"**[53] (Grades K-5) Young children try to find pairs of photographs of their group members placed face down on a table. Teaches children to recognize the members of the group, their names and their diversity, and gives them practice actively assisting others to succeed.

2. **"Thumbs-Up and Thumbs-Down Displays"**[54] (Grades K-5) Children illustrate examples of positive (thumbs-up) and negative (thumbs-down) behaviors on two separate bulletin boards.

3. **"The Vougeville Dress Code Disaster"**[55] (Grades 6-8) Students working in groups to negotiate their assigned "demands" concerning dress codes in their schools with other groups that have been assigned other conflicting "demands." The negotiation is followed by a discussion of how the role-play escalated towards conflict and de-escalated towards a more peaceful discussion as people attempted to keep the discussion on track.

4. **"The Lorax"**[56] (Grades 6-8) Youth consider the conflicts that are brought up in Dr. Seuss's story *The Lorax*. After reading the story, they discuss the uses of resources and people's responsibilities for environmental problems. At the end of the discussion, youths play roles in a town meeting trying to address conflicts between environmentalists and manufacturers.

5. **"The Discrimination Collage"**[57] (Grades 6-8) Youth are broken up into small groups. Each group is given different materials to use in making a collage that depicts stereotyping. If the groups complain about unfairness in regards to the differences in materials distributed, they are simply told that "That is just the way life is." Near the end of the process, youth are asked to reveal through discussion how they felt as they worked, how it looked the other teams were handling it, and what lessons they can draw.

[53-54] Sample activity from: *Adventures in Peacemaking: A Conflict Resolution Guide*. Cambridge: Educators for Social Responsibility. 1995.

[55-57] Sample activity from: *Conflict Resolution in the Middle School*. Cambridge: Educators for Social Responsibility. 1997.

6. **"Human Treasure Hunt"**[58] Players use a "treasure hunt" list of facts to find matches with other people in the group (items such as "is born in the same month as you," "has been in a parade," etc.).

7. **"Trust Circle"**[59] Arrange children in a circle with one person standing in the center, palms raised, facing outwards. As this person slowly walks to the edges, eyes closed, waiting participants carefully guide the center person to another place in the circle.

8. **"Python Pentathlon"**[60] Players sit in an L-shaped balanced position that has the player's feet and head off the ground. Players attempt to move forward or backward on command. Once experienced, the players then form small teams where each player sits immediately behind another player, placing his or her feet and lower legs in the lap of the person in front of them. Only the first and last person in the line can have foot or hand contact with the ground. The object is for each team to "walk" on their bottoms to a specified destination without coming apart.

[56-59] Sample activity from Quicksilver: Adventure Games, *Initiative Problems, Trust Activities, and a Guide to Effective Leadership*. Adapted and reprinted ©Project Adventure by permission. (See Additional Social Competence Resources.)

[60] Sample activity from *Cowstails and Cobras II: A Guide to Games, Initiatives, Ropes Courses and Adventure Curriculum*. Adapted and reprinted ©Project Adventure by permission. (See Additional Social Competence Resources.)

Section 6

Additional Social-Competence Resources

1. **Bringing Yourself to Work: Caregiving in After-School Environments** is a training model for after-school program staff that enables after-school caregivers to integrate self-knowledge and personal experience into their relationships with adults and children. **www.bringingyourselftowork.com**

2. **Collaborative for Academic, Emotional, and Social Learning** (CASEL) provide guidelines, tools, informational resources and support to practitioners seeking to improve and expand their social-emotional learning (SEL) programming. **www.casel.org/home/index.php**

3. **Educators for Social Responsibility** (ESR) curriculum and activity books (*Adventures in Peacemaking: A Conflict Resolution Guide for School-Age Programs and Conflict Resolution in the Middle-School*) are comprehensive, contain varied activities and are thoroughly researched, well written and well tested in the field. The activity guides address social and emotional learning, conflict resolution and diversity education with the intention of helping to build caring learning environments and pro-social children. ESR's research indicates that programs that regularly use their programs foster children who work harder to solve problems in non-violent ways and perform well on their academic achievement tests. **www.esrnational.org**

4. **Open Circle** works with school communities to foster the development of relationships that support safe, caring and respectful learning communities and help children become ethical people, contributing citizens and successful learners. **www.open-circle.org**

5. **Project Adventure, Inc.** publishes books and educational material for the field of adventure workshops, games and activities, which include challenge ropes courses, trust activities and cooperative sports and games. Activities for pre-school through elementary and middle-school grades, as well as adult learners, can be found in Project Adventure Activity guides. **www.pa.org**

Recommended Reading

1. Schwartz, Wendy. *Developing Social-Competence in Children*. New York: Teachers College Press. 1999.
    http://iume.tc.columbia.edu/choices/briefs/choices03.html

2. McClellan, Diane E. *Assessing Young Children's Social-Competence.* ERIC Digests. 2003-04. www.ericdigests.org/2001-4/assessing.html

Fitness and Nutrition

Being fit and well fed results in what is commonly referred to as wellness. To be "well" is to have good health, heart and breathing endurance, flexibility, muscular strength and endurance, good nutritional habits, psycho-emotional strength and an appropriate weight/height ratio. In after-school programs, the games, events and activities associated with eating and physical activity contribute to fitness and nutritional health and also serve as opportunities for children and youth to develop social skills.

Why Include Fitness and Nutrition in After-School Programs?

An individual who is fit has heart and breathing endurance, muscular strength and flexibility. After-school programs that include activities which result in children and youth using their muscles, raising their heart and breathing rates and using a full range of motion at the joints, can contribute to children's overall fitness and wellness.

> **Heart and Breathing Endurance** concerns the efficient functioning of the heart and lungs before, during and after exercise. In general, once physical activity begins and is continued in a regular fashion throughout one's lifetime, heart and breathing endurance develop and can be sustained.

> **Muscular Strength and Endurance** concerns how much work a muscle can do, and how long before it can no longer move the body as desired. Increasing the amount of time a muscle is asked to work develops endurance. Physical activity develops both strength and endurance.

> **Flexibility** concerns the range of motion at the body's joints. The hips, shoulders, elbows, wrists, knees, ankle and back are the major body joints. Maintaining flexibility is important for preventing injury. Increasing strength of muscles associated with any joint while maintaining the range of motion inherent in that joint maintains flexibility at the joint.

Nutrition concerns itself with the quality, frequency and amount of food eaten each day by an individual. Being active and eating well contribute to an individual's wellness. Good nutritional habits begin in the home. After-school programs that both model good nutritional habits and provide healthy food choices contribute to good nutritional habits and overall wellness.

Section 6

What Can Children and Youth Learn from Fitness and Nutrition Activities?

Fitness:
- The kinds of exercise which provide a total body workout and build heart and breathing endurance, muscle strength, and endurance and flexibility.
- The amounts of exercise which are good for building strength, endurance and flexibility.
- Ways of exercising which are fun and can be done with others.
- How to be one's own physical trainer.

Nutrition:
- What foods to eat.
- How much of each food group to eat.
- How to be a good role model for others.
- How to prepare healthy foods or meals.
- How eating well and exercising regularly develop wellness and optimize growth.

Three Fitness and Nutrition Concepts

MOVE MORE After-school programs create schedules and facilities that optimize physical movement and physically active lifestyles.

Example: Programs regularly include large muscle and group games, physical exercise or team sports and fitness-related or active service-learning projects.

THINK HEALTHY Children and youth learn to make healthy, informed decisions about exercise and diet.

Example: After-school programs are filled with healthy role models and accessible fitness and nutrition resources. Programs are respectful, caring, secure and emotionally safe places for children and youth to be.

EAT SMART Students and staff have access to nutritious, healthy foods, and they eat well as a result of education and personal example.

Example: Cafeterias, vending machines and sports events provide nutritional foods. Colorful posters advocate wise food choices and programs include nutrition-related activities and counseling.

Age and Development

Maturation, genetics and nutrition all play significant roles in determining levels of fitness and wellness for an individual throughout his or her lifetime. Because of these variables, it is difficult to set firm standards for fitness or nutritional habits for broad age groups, or to even chart progression from "unfit" to "fit" in any precise manner. Changes in fitness, nutrition and wellness are better calculated on an individual basis rather than at a group level. However, the National Association for Sport and Physical Education has defined standards for learning that can be applied to planning activities associated with fitness development in children and youth. Benchmarks for nutrition activities are also generally agreed upon. (See Section 4 for sample fitness and nutrition benchmarks.)

Daily Schedule

Unfortunately, whether due to budget constraints or concern about standardized tests, many schools are increasingly narrowing their curricula to academic subjects and forgoing opportunities to teach children the critical life skills of good nutrition and fitness. After-school programs are ideally suited to incorporate these critical developmental needs into their daily and weekly schedules. The daily schedule of any after-school program must include time for physical activity and nutrition, if only in the "free time" when children and youth can run around outside or in a gym, or in the snacks served by the program.

Beyond these obvious opportunities, there are myriad ways to incorporate fitness and nutrition activities into a program. Children and youth who are eager and interested in sports should be given opportunities to hone their skills after-school since other opportunities may be limited. It is just as important to encourage and expose children and youth who are not inclined towards sports to engage in physical activity, to help them develop skills, confidence and lifelong healthful habits. Exposing children and youth on a daily basis to healthy foods and activities that strengthen their understanding of good nutrition is also critical to their optimal development.

Section 6

Sample Fitness Activity Plan

Title

Track Meet Project

Description

Plan and organize a field and track event involving children and youth, staff and families.

Objectives

Engage children and youth in active learning that enhances their physical fitness, social-competence and problem-solving skills.

Intended Outcomes

- Children and youth will improve their physical fitness and learn about the relationship between nutrition, fitness and good health.
- Children and youth will learn to work together towards a common goal.
- Children and youth will gain experience reading, writing, speaking and listening.
- Children and youth will learn to solve problems using tools of computation and estimation.

Special Materials and Tools

Team shirts, batons, prizes, hurdles, shot puts.

Special Space Requirements

Indoor or outdoor track.

Ages/Group Size

This activity could engage everyone in the program, with age-appropriate involvement.

The Activity

Brainstorm with children and youth what they know about track meets, what activities they would like to compete in, etc. (Use K/W/L chart) Conduct research and interviews to learn more. Plan track meet events, participation, rules, etc.

Train/learn specific events. Work towards "personal best" goals.

Set the stage – permissions, prizes, dates, publicity, officials, etc.

(see Track Meet Project web for ideas of how the activity might unfold)

Incorporating Technology

- Research relevant age-specific benchmarks for various track events to help set goals, create training regimens, etc.
- Create website to post information about the events, schedules, results, etc.

Extensions and Continuations

The track meet could be an annual or semi-annual event.

Children and youth could learn about the effects of nutrition and rest on athletic performance.

Conclusions/Reflections

See how training affected individual performance – attaining "personal best" goals, etc.

What aspect of the meet did children enjoy most – training, competing, publicizing, etc.?

Documentation

Photos of training activities, track events, posted records and "personal best" times, distances, etc.

Links to Learning: *A Curriculum Planning Guide for After-School Programs*

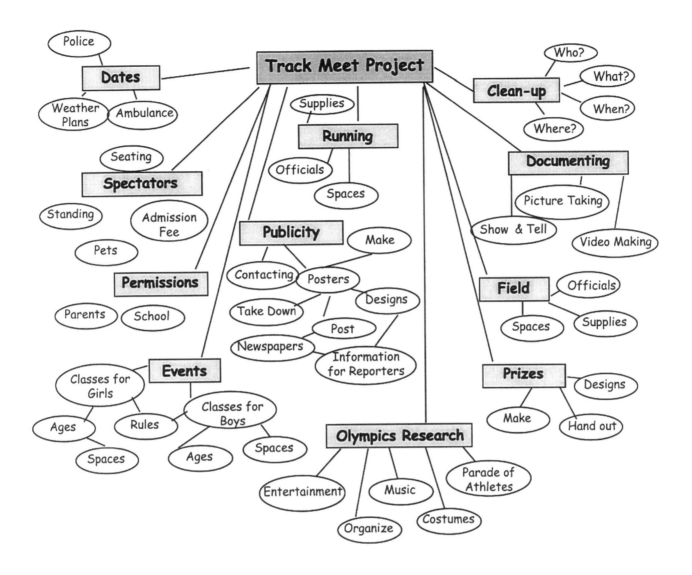

Linking to Quality Standards and Learning Benchmarks

Activity Title	Track Meet Project						
Description	Plan and organize a track meet involving children and youth, staff and families.						

Core Content Area (check all that apply)	Math	Literacy	Science	Arts	Fitness/ Nutrition	Social Competence	Other
	✓	✓	✓		✓	✓	

Skills for the New Economy (check all that apply)	Numeracy	Communication		Problem solving	Technology	Work w/others
	✓	✓		✓		✓

Quality Standards	**NAA** #4 – Staff interact with children to help them learn #13 – Activities reflect the mission of the program and promote the development of all children #28 – Staff and children work together to plan suitable activities	**SACERS**	**OTHER** Search Institute's 40 Developmental Assets #17- Creative activities: encourage children to develop their unique talents #23 - Stimulating activity: encourage children to explore and engage in stimulating activity

	Standard	**Grade/Age**	**Description**
Benchmark or Learning Standard	National Content Standards for Physical Education	K-12	1. Demonstrates proficiency in a few movement forms 2. Achieves and maintains a health-enhancing level of physical fitness 3. Understands that physical activity provides opportunities for enjoyment, challenge, self-expression and social interaction
Benchmark or Learning Standard	CASEL Social Emotional Learning Competencies	N/A	Self-management: goal setting Decision making: analyzing situations, respecting others, problem solving Relationship skills: communication, building relationships, negotiation
Benchmark or Learning Standard	Standards for Language Arts (4th Ed.) Mid-continent Research for Education and Language	Grade 6	Reading: make connections between characters and events in text with people or events in own life Writing: write to address problems, respond to literature, express ideas, and evaluate

Benchmark or Learning Standard	Standards for Mathematics (4th Ed.) Mid-continent Research for Education and Language	Grades 5-8	<u>Number and number relationships</u>: understand basic number concepts for whole numbers, fractions, decimals, integers and rational numbers <u>Statistics</u>: understand that data represents pieces of information about objects or activities, use data and statistical measures, organize data using tables, graphs and frequency distributions, and read and interpret tables, plots and charts

Additional Fitness and Nutrition Resources

Fitness
Grades K - 6

1. Whitaker, David L. *Games, Games, Games: Creating Hundreds of Group Games and Sports*. Nashville: School-Age NOTES.1996. www.AfterSchoolCatalog.com

2. Sanders, Stephen W. *Active for Life:Developmentally Appropriate Movement Programs for Young Children*. Washington, DC: NAEYC. 2002. www.naeyc.org

3. Weikart, Phyllis S. *Round the Circle: Key Experiences in Movement for Young Children, and Movement in Steady Beat: Activities for Children Ages 3 to7*. Ypsilanti, MI: High Scope Publishing. 2000. www.highscope.org

4. Weikart, Phyllis S. and Elizabeth B. Carlton. *85 Engaging Movement Activities – Learning on the Move*. Ypsilanti, MI: High Scope Publishing. 2000. www.highscope.org

5. Kogut, S.P. (Ed.). *Beyond Activities: Learning Experiences to Support the National Physical Education Standards, Elementary,* PreK to 5. From The American Alliance for Health, Physical Education, Recreation, and Dance. www.aahperd.org

6. LeFevre, Dale B. *Best New Games*. Champaign, IL: Human Kinetics Press. 2002.

7. "Wellness & Nutrition: Get Physical." The Quaker Oats Company. Articles with activity ideas such as: How to Be Fit on a Busy Schedule; Enjoy The Great Outdoors; Have A Ball? Play On The Ball!; Changing Seasons and Changing Exercise; Tips for Keeping Fit over the Holidays; and Sample Workout for Beginning Exercisers. www.quakeroatmeal.com/Wellness/GetPhysical

Section 6

8. Clements, Rhonda L., Ed.D, (Ed). *Elementary School Recess: Selected Readings, Games, and Activities for Teachers and Parents*. American Press. 2000. Articles that detail the benefits of recess and play to children's physical, mental and emotional well being. Also full descriptions of many old favorite playground games such as "Duck, Duck, Goose," "Kickball," "RedLight" and "Simon Says." www.AfterSchoolCatalog.com

Grades 6 - 12

1. Franks, B., et al. *The Health Fitness Handbook*. Champaign, IL: Human Kinetics Press. 2003. Everything you will need to start a safe, effective fitness program or to make existing programs better. www.humankinetics.com

2. Mohnsen, Bonnie (Ed.). *Concepts and Principles of Physical Education: What Every Student Needs to Know*. Champaign, IL: Human Kinetics Press, 2003. Includes the National Standards for Physical Education, as well as examples, lessons and assessment ideas. www.humankinetics.com or www.aahperd.org

3. Centers for Disease Control. *Promoting Physical Activity: A Guide for Community Action*. Champaign, IL: Human Kinetics Press, 1999. Guidelines for promoting physical activity among young people are thoroughly described. www.humankinetics.com

4. Centers for Disease Control. *Active Youth: Ideas for Implementing CDC Physical Activity Promotion Guidelines*. Champaign, IL: Human Kinetics Press. 1998. Examples and descriptions of effective programs that address the CDC guide lines for promoting physical activity among young people. www.humankinetics.com.

5. Kogut, S.P. (Ed.). *Beyond Activities – Secondary Edition*. Middle – High School Grades, from the American Alliance for Health, Physical Education, Recreation, and Dance. www.aahperd.org

6. Decker, June and Monica Maze. *Walking Games and Activities*. Champaign, IL: Human Kinetics Press. 2002. Combine the concepts of fitness and walking with games. Lesson plans and activity ideas are included. www.humankinetics.com

Nutrition
Grades K - 5

1. Thonney, P.F. & T. J. Farrell. *Kitchen Science for Kids*. New York: Cornell University Cooperative. 1995. Available from www.redleafpress.org

2. Appleton, J., et al. *Do Carrots Make You See Better?: A Guide to Food and Nutrition in Early Childhood Programs*. PreK to 3. Beltsville, MD: Gryphon House. 2001.

3. MacDonald, Sharon and Marilee Harrald-Pilz. *Idea Bags for the Kitchen: Activities to Promote the School-Home Connection.* PreK to 3. Fearon Teachers Aids. 2002. Available from www.redleafpress.org

4. The Quaker Oats Company, "Kids' Food Pyramid", "Quaker Oatmeal, Strive for Five" (5-step family nutrition program). www.quakeroatmeal.com

5. University of California, Cooperative Extension, Fresno County, Youth Nutrition Education Programs. Four free nutrition education curriculum guides supporting the California Content Standards in Math, English, Science, Grades, Pre-School to grade 8. http://cefresno.ucdavis.edu/EFNEP253/

6. Food and Nutrition Information Center, Kids' Sites – Activities for Children, Food and Nutrition Fun Games and Activities and other government related sites and resources. www.nal.usda.gov/fnic/etext/000100.html

7. "Scope and Sequence for Youth Nutrition Curriculum." For PreK to fifth grade. Knowledge objectives, behaviored objectives, sample activities for Food Guide Pyramid use; Food and meal selection activities; Physical activity; Food safety activities. http://fnp.ifas.ufl.edu

Grades 6 - 12

1. CanFit, 2140 Shattuck Ave. Suite 610, Berkeley, CA 94704. Nutrition related activities and the home of *PHAT – Promoting Healthy Activities Together*, nutrition and physical activity ideas. www.canfit.org/html/nutrition_activities.html

2. YourSELF Middle School Nutrition Education Kit, at www.usda.gov/fcs/team/teamnutr.htm, Cornell University, www.cce.cornell.edu/programs/food/staff/at07898/children.html Helps 7th and 8th graders make smart choices about eating and physical activity. Contains student workbooks, duplication masters, videos, YourSELF magazine, posters and ideas for linking cafeteria and classroom.

3. "Fun 4-H Activities with Food," Michigan State University Extension, http://www.msue.msu.edu/cyf/youth/foodactiv.htm

4. Youth-Health Nutrition, at www.youth-health.com/Nutrition.html A collection of links to websites devoted to youth and nutrition.

Technology

Computers, digital cameras, video-recorders, scanners – all these technologies and more are increasingly embraced by staff and children alike in out-of-school-time programs. Sometimes programs have access to a computer lab in a school; sometimes they create their own technology centers because parents, youth or staff members express an interest in using computers after school. Although computers and other technology are more and more prevalent in informal settings, effectively designing and implementing technology-enriched after-school programs is a complex challenge.

Ideally, the goal of incorporating technology into an after-school program is not to teach "technology" as a discrete subject, but rather to use technology in learning activities that enable students to connect their academic learning with experiences that are relevant and meaningful for them. In other words, technology should be used as a tool for learning – not an end in itself. Multi-dimensional project-based activities are especially well suited for this approach to incorporating technology.

This section provides a broad overview and some basic information about how to incorporate technology into your program in this manner. For more detailed guidance, the YouthLearn manual and website are highly recommended.[61] These resources provide step-by-step lessons, worksheets, guidelines and other tools that can help you create high quality after-school programs that incorporate technology effectively.

Why Include Technology in After-School Programs?

Murname and Levy included "knowledge and comfort with technology"[62] as one of their six "New Basic Skills" young people need in order to succeed in today's economy. Fortunately, in addition to being a critical skill for employment, computers and related technology also have the virtue of being highly attractive and intriguing to most children and youth, regardless of their academic proclivities. As such, technology can be a tremendously powerful tool to engage children in learning, even students who have encountered difficulties in traditional academic settings.

Children's desire to access various technologies can be a powerful motivator, spurring them to new levels of engagement with traditional subjects such as reading and math. For many, the speed and breadth of the Internet and its mysteries can make inquiry and discovery – the central components of science – an absorbing adventure. Incorporated into the right project-based activities, technology can also be a valuable way to build children's social competencies by providing problem-solving environments in which they can develop teamwork and other social skills. Finally, the success and achievement children and youth experience with technology-enriched activities can give many of them new confidence in their own strengths and broaden their life goals.

---

[61] This chapter was written in collaboration with Education Development Center, Inc. and relies on material from the YouthLearn Initiative. *The YouthLearn Guide: A Creative Approach to Working with Youth and Technology* provides general guidance on inquiry-based project planning and management, as well as specific and detailed instruction on ways to incorporate technology-rich activities into out-of-school-time programs. Copies of the guide can be purchased through EDC: 800-449-5525 or at www.youthlearn.org.

[62] By technology, Murname and Levy mean computers and other electronic machines and devices. Frank Levy and Richard J. Murname, *The New Basic Skills*, Free Press, 1996.

The Power of Technology

One after-school program in Washington, DC used resources they found on the Internet to test the quality of the water flowing into their homes and in the nearby Anacostia River. After writing up their results on computer spreadsheets, the students compared what they found with government water-quality standards. Then, using the Internet and their newly stoked curiosity about the chemistry of water, they began to learn about the Clean Water Act, which was pending authorization in Congress. Many of the students lived within two miles of the Capitol, but this was the first time they felt connected to the work inside that ornate domed building – and the first time they realized that they could become active participants in their community.

— From the YouthLearn Initiative at EDC

Integrating Technology Effectively

Creating meaningful after-school projects that take full advantage of the unique learning opportunities that computers and other technology can afford requires a great deal of time, thought and care. The most successful programs have the following "core components":

- At least one full-time staff person dedicated to overseeing technology-related activities.

- Full integration of all staff who work on technology-related projects with other program staff – for planning, training and other program development and management activities.

- A dedicated space with at least 15 networked workstations, a high-speed Internet connection, software appropriate for project-based instruction and related equipment such as digital cameras and printers.

In addition to these basic requirements, programs need to provide ongoing support to staff. This support includes technical support for hardware and software troubleshooting and access to training and other forms of professional development specific to technology-enriched learning.

Section 6

Media Literacy

In our media-saturated world, kids are constantly bombarded by messages, images, opinions and ideas. Add the Internet, Web, email and wireless devices into the mix, and it's difficult for any of us to escape the information – and misinformation – glut. It is increasingly important to teach the critical skills of analyzing messages and information for validity and bias. Analyzing and evaluating sources is an essential part of all inquiry-based learning projects, but our multimedia world means that we have to teach kids not just how to assess data and arguments, but also how to discern emotional appeals made through pictures, music, and video. Helping kids become wise consumers of information is a fundamental component of integrating technology effectively as a tool for learning. Toward this end, there is a vast array of media literacy resources freely available for educators online.

— From the YouthLearn Initiative at EDC

Other important tips to keep in mind when working with children and technology include:

- Start with what children and youth know – Find out what the children and youth already know about the technology you are using. You are likely to discover a wide range of comfort and experience. Knowing where the participants start out will help you tailor the learning to their needs and will also allow you to capitalize on the "experts" in your audience, giving more knowledgeable youth a chance to shine and others a chance to learn from their peers.

- Integrate goals – Ensure that all technology-related activities are fully integrated with your program's mission, goals and objectives. New technology should always be introduced in the context of a larger project, not as an end in itself. For example, teach a web-authoring tool in the context of developing a website that children want to create. All activities should also clearly relate back to the learning benchmarks or quality standards that your program adheres to.

- Start simple – Before you engage with a new technology, make sure the students understand basic concepts. For example, before you use a computerized drawing program, teach basic drawing techniques with paper and crayons or markers. Once children have mastered certain concepts or technologies, allow them to build on that knowledge and expand it.

- Expect problems – Technology can be temperamental. Expect that you may have difficulties with hardware, software, connections, etc. Make the fact and the manner of overcoming these problems part of the learning process; children will learn valuable lessons about persistence, good humor, safeguards, collaboration, etc. from your example.

- Leave room for creativity – As with any child-directed learning, leave room for children's ideas to shape the outcome of your projects and activities. Often they will have ideas that you have never thought of. Opportunities for them to engage their curiosity and imagination are the best learning experiences they can have.

Online Safety for Children and Youth

Along with the wonders of cyberspace, there are, unfortunately, some risks. Risks include both individuals who might seek to exploit or harm children and exposure to materials that are inappropriate for children. Fears of these potential downsides should not discourage after-school programs from taking advantage of the Internet. Adapting and extending your program's general safety precautions to online activities – and providing positive, constructive and meaningful activities that are carefully supervised – are the best safety measures that you can implement. For more information about protecting children's safety and privacy online, visit the Federal Trade Commission's website at: http://www.ftc.gov/bcp/conline/pubs/online/teachers.htm

— From the YouthLearn Initiative at EDC

Environment

Most programs that conduct technology-rich activities will have access to a discrete room or space dedicated to computers and other technology – a computer lab or technology center. A well thought-out design of this space helps make the most of the equipment and allows instructors to manage groups effectively. The following are a few basic guidelines for the design and maintenance of your center:

- Make sure the room has good lighting and ample space and is secure. Ideally, the room will have space for activities that are part of a project but do not use the computers – e.g. tables for writing or drawing, meeting space for discussions or teamwork, as well as storage for on-going work and space for peripheral equipment such as printers, cameras, etc.

- Machines should be located around the perimeter of the room or on an interior "island" allowing the instructor to move easily around the room to monitor activities and provide assistance. Leave at least 18 inches between machines to allow space for children's books and papers or to enable two children to share a computer during collaborative work.

- Furnish the center with ergonomic, adjustable tables and chairs that can safely accommodate all the different sizes, shapes and needs of the children and youth you serve.

Daily Schedule

Most technology centers are in high demand during after-school hours. Some programs try to schedule every age group in the center daily, even if that means that the time is short and everyone feels rushed. Creating a schedule that provides different age groups with fewer sessions per week but with longer blocks of time gives both staff and children better opportunities to delve into their projects and transition in and out of the center.

Try to group children of the same age range together and schedule instructors to work with the age group they are most effective and comfortable with. If staff constraints are such that staff must work with a very wide age range, try to concentrate similar ages or developmental groups on the same days, i.e. pre-teens and teens on Mondays and 5-6 and 7-8 year-olds on Tuesdays, etc. Finally, given the research that shows the importance of providing teens with constructive after-school alternatives to drugs, crime and other dangerous activities, make sure the center is available to them during some of these key hours.

Section 6

Age and Development

In general, grouping children of similar ages or skill levels together is the most effective way to conduct technology-related activities. Groups with common reading and writing abilities, similar understanding of concepts or subject areas, and comparable abilities in negotiating social interactions, allow the instructor to focus on common needs and manage activities smoothly.

There is a current debate about the value of computer use among very young children. Critics feel that very young children should concentrate on developing their gross motor and social skills and follow their natural curiosity in ways that are not subject to the constraints inherent in computers. Others feel that it is important for children to master technology at an early age so as not to fall behind their peers. Your program should determine what kinds of technology, if any, you wish to include in programs you offer young children.[63]

---

[63] For more on this debate, you may wish to review the following article: Paul Attewell, Belkis Suazo-Gracia and Juan Battle, "Computers and Young Children: Social Benefit or Social Problem?" in *Social Forces*, September 2003, 82(1):277-296, ©The University of North Carolina Press. www.gc.cuny.edu/studies/attewell03.pdf

Sample Technology Activity Plan

Title

What's the Weather? Creating a Simple Web Page [64]

Description

Introduces youth to basic web-page design and creates a site that they can check for information every day to gain experience being online.

Objectives

Provide technology, literacy, science, arts and social competence activities.

Intended Outcomes

- Children will gain experience with graphics and web-page authoring software and practice Internet navigation.
- Children will gain experience and practice reading, writing, speaking and listening.
- Children will gain new understanding of weather prediction and data gathering and management.
- Children will express new understanding/knowledge through a variety of media including writing, drawing and web design.
- Children will gain experience working with others to increase knowledge and solve problems.

Special Materials and Tools

Computers with Internet connections, Web page-authoring software, graphics software.

Space Requirements

Discussion area and tables to work on.

Age/Group Size

Appropriate for ages 9-11. This project could involve 5-20 children.

The Activity

- Find the data sources – Either have the kids search for sites themselves or create your own simple site with a handful of links to potential data sources (such as the Weather Channel or USA Today).
- Create the graphics – Keep the graphics simple but introduce drawing software and/or take photos or scan pictures.
- Create the Web page – Introduce web-authoring tools and demonstrate how to add text, images and links.

Incorporating Technology

Since this is a "technology" activity, think about ways to extend into other key learning areas such as arts (add music to the website), math (analyze weather data from two locations and create comparison charts and tables) or fitness (how do weather changes affect opportunities or safety of physical activities?).

Extensions and Continuations

Choose other topics to focus on for your website. Be sure to select information that changes every day, such as local sports scores, front page headlines or stock prices. In addition, keep in mind that you want to be able to compare at least two related data points.

---

[64] For a more detailed description of this project see the YouthLearn website:
www.youthlearn.org/learning/activities/multimedia/weather.asp

Section 6

Conclusions/Reflections

Hold discussions with children about what they learned about the differences in weather in two locations and how the technology helped or hindered their understanding and ability to communicate their knowledge.

Documentation

The website serves as a final "document" to display the project.

Linking to Quality Standards and Learning Benchmarks

Activity Title	What's the Weather? Creating a Simple Web Page						
Description	Introduces youth to basic web page design and creates a site that they can check for information every day to gain experience being online.						

Core Content Area (check all that apply)	Math	Literacy	Science	Arts	Fitness/ Nutrition	Social Competence	Other
		✓	✓	✓		✓	

Skills for the New Economy (check all that apply)	Numeracy	Communication		Problem solving	Technology	Work w/others
		✓		✓	✓	✓

Quality Standards	**NAA**	**SACERS**	**OTHER**
	#4 – Staff interact with children to help them learn #14 – Activities reflect the mission of the program and promote the development of children	26. Science and Nature Activities– Staff extend children's interest and introduce new concepts	Search Institute's 40 Developmental Assets #22 - young person actively engaged in learning

	Standard	Grade/Age	Description
Benchmark or Learning Standard	ISTENETS Technology Foundation Standards	N/A	Basic operations and concepts – demonstrate a sound understanding of the nature and operation of technology systems. Technology communication tools – use a variety of media and formats to communicate information and ideas Technology research tools – use technology to locate, evaluate and collect information from a variety of sources.
Benchmark or Learning Standard	Standards for Language Arts (4th Ed.) Mid-continent Research for Education and Language	Grade 3 Grade 6	• Establish purpose for reading (e.g. fun, information, understand varying points of view) • Use a variety of strategies to create writing (e.g. draft outline, brainstorming, research topic) • Use reading skills to understand a variety of informational texts, draw conclusions and make inferences from text • Use various strategies to edit written work
Benchmark or Learning Standard	Standards for Science (4th Ed.) Mid-continent Research for Education and Language	Grades 6-8	Research Skills - use online databases to locate sources; organize information and ideas in systemic ways, use appropriate methods to cite sources

Section 6

Benchmark or Learning Standard	ArtsEdge National Standards for Arts Education	N/A	Production and performance: understand art as a venue for communicating ideas and meanings; connect and compare various art forms.
Benchmark or Learning Standard	Social Competence	N/A	Relationship skills: communication, building relationships, negotiation

Other Sample Technology Activities [65]

1. **The Soil Around Us** (ages 9-11) Introduces methods for investigating the origins, characteristics and uses of soil, building on this age group's innate curiosity about the natural world. Can be adapted to other age groups by modifying reading material, group activities, etc.

2. **Internet Photo Essays** (ages 12-16) Participants will formulate questions about social issues and events. Computer-based activities emphasize multimedia skills, such as creating and editing graphics and text, and introduce basic Internet skills, such as using email and search engines. Project introduces collaborative group work processes such as mapping and storyboarding and participants learn how to build a Web page.

3. **Four Out of Five Kids Surveyed: Conducting a Survey and Creating a Web Page** (ages 10-14) Kids do a quick survey on a topic of their choice, take photos to illustrate their findings and build a Web page with the results.

4. **Build Your Own Zoo: An Inspiration Project to Introduce Presentations** (ages 7-9) *Inspiration* is a software program that helps people organize their thoughts and make simple presentations. In this project, you'll introduce kids to the basic features of *Inspiration* and have them create a web map to present ideas for their own zoo.

5. **Zany Zoom Ins: Fun With Close-Up Photographs** (ages 10-14) Even if you're introducing photography as part of a larger project, you'll want to spend time over several sessions introducing photographic techniques to kids to help them understand elementary concepts like distance, angle and framing. "Zany Zoom Ins" is an intermediate activity you can use along the way. In this activity, the kids take ultra-close-up photographs of common objects to identify what they are.

---

[65] All of these activity ideas can be found on the YouthLearn website where they are accompanied by detailed lesson planning advice: www.youthlearn.org/learning/activities/index.html

Additional Technology Resources

1. **The Global Schoolhouse** brings together opportunities for conducting projects using the Internet and working collaboratively with schools across the world. It contains a project registry with over 900 online projects and conducts an annual competition among schools and youth organizations around the world to conduct research and publish their findings on the Web. **www.globalschoolnet.org/index.html**

2. **Log On and Learn More: Ten Online Projects to Enhance Your Curriculum** This article focuses on helping teachers integrate technology into the classroom without losing valuable teaching time. The projects described are linked and include contacting email pen pals, watching weather and researching huskies. Numerous resources are listed to help each project along. **www.education-world.com/a_curr/curr164.shtml**

3. **The International Education and Resource Network (iEARN)** is a non-profit global network that enables young people to use the Internet and other new technologies to engage in collaborative educational projects that both enhance learning and make a difference in the world. Participants may join existing structured online projects, or work with others internationally to create and facilitate their own projects to fit their particular classroom and curriculum needs. **www.iearn.org**

4. **The Internet Public Library (IPL)** is an online library at the University of Michigan School of Information which has a section devoted to children called Kidspace. Kidspace has links to abundant links and resources for kids, teachers and parents, including many reference tools typically found in libraries. **www.ipl.org/kidspace**

5. **ThinkQuest** is an international competition where student teams engage in collaborative, project-based learning to create educational websites. The winning entries form the ThinkQuest online library containing links to over 5,000 student-created sites. **www.thinkquest.org**

6. **The YouthLearn Initiative at Education Development Center** features lesson plans, techniques and tips on curriculum design, and other resources for learning programs, with an emphasis on project-based learning and technology integration. In addition to the website and The YouthLearn Guide, YouthLearn also offers a database of additional resources and a discussion list for youth development practitioners. **www.youthlearn.org**

7. **Youth Net: Interactive Projects for Grades K-12.** This website links to a number of great online Web-based projects on a wide variety of topics. The projects are complete and well thought out and all incorporate some form of interactive media or an online activity. **http://youth.net/**

Recommended Reading

e-Learning: Putting a World-Class Education at the Fingertips of All Children This document, the National Educational Technology Plan of the U.S. Department of Education, (2000) outlines research and evaluation regarding the integration of technology into teaching. http://www.air.org/pdf/e-learning.pdf

Section 6

Discussion Questions for Section Six

1. Which of the selected content areas are your favorites? Why are they your favorites?

2. What is it like when you need to get kids involved with an area that is not one of your favorites? How can you ensure that kids can be enthusiastic and engaged even if it is not your favorite topic/activity?

3. Select an activity, project or program improvement idea from this guide (or any other resource) that stretches you to try something new. Plan to implement it in your program using the following planning tools.

Planning Questions:

   a. What specific idea(s) do you want to implement at your site? (e.g. activities, changes in space, policy, or program structure, improved staff/child relationships, community awareness, etc.)

   b. What are your goals for this activity/project/program improvement? (Think about goals related to children doing the activities you choose, e.g. what they might experience, learn, practice, or improve by doing them.)

   c. As a result of implementing these ideas, what changes do you expect to see in the children, youth or staff? (e.g. skills development, change in staff practices or attitude.) What challenges/barriers might you face in implementing these ideas? What specific strategies come to mind for addressing these challenges?

   d. Create an action plan that indicates the steps you'll take to implement your idea(s). What needs to be done? Who will do each task? What is the time frame for each step?

Reflection/Assessment Questions:

After implementing your activity/project/program improvement idea(s), answer the following questions:

   a. What was the child, youth or staff response to the idea(s) you implemented?

   b. What were the positive outcomes of yours and/or their efforts? How can you sustain, extend or build on the idea(s) and what worked well?

   c. What were the challenges that arose that made implementation of the idea(s) difficult? How were they addressed?

   d. What might you do differently next time?

Appendix A: General Resources

National Organizations and Initiatives

Academy for Educational Development (AED) is an independent, non-profit organization committed to solving critical social problems in the U.S. and throughout the world through education, social marketing, research, training, policy analysis and innovative program design and management. Major areas of focus include health, education, youth development and the environment. **www.aed.org/**

Adolescence Directory On-Line (ADOL) is an electronic guide to information on adolescent issues. Educators, counselors, parents, researchers, health practitioners and teens can use ADOL to find Web resources for topics concerning adolescents. **http://education.indiana.edu/cas/adol/adol.html**

Afterschool Alliance is an alliance of public, private and non-profit groups committed to raising awareness and expanding resources for after-school programs. Initiated and currently coordinated by the C.S. Mott Foundation, the Alliance grew out of a partnership between the Foundation and the U.S. Department of Education. **www.afterschoolalliance.org**

Center for Youth Development and Policy Research (CYDPR) The Center's mission is to create and strengthen the infrastructures that support positive development for all youth in America. Activities include public education, research, policy formulation and technical assistance aimed at U.S. communities that seek to expand opportunities and support systems for disadvantaged young people. **www.aed.org/us/youth.html**

Center for Social and Emotional Education is a non-profit, international organization that helps youth prepare for healthy, responsible and productive lives by using social and emotional education to help transform problems into opportunities. It also provides parents and educators with resources and tools that promote social and emotional skills and knowledge in our children and adolescents. **www.csee.net**

Child Care Aware is a non-profit initiative whose mission is to ensure that every parent has access to good information about finding quality child care and resources in their community, through national consumer marketing and by raising visibility for local child care resource and referral agencies. **www.childcareaware.org**

Child Trends is a non-profit, non-partisan research organization dedicated to studying children, youth and families through research, data collection and data analyses. **www.childtrends.org**

Corporation for National Service (CNS) provides information on federal programs that benefit children and youth such as AmeriCorps, Learn & Serve, America Reads and National Service Scholarships. **www.nationalservice.org**

CYFER-net, or Children Youth Family Educational Research Network, provides hundreds of complete on-line publications featuring practical, research based information on children, youth and families. **www.cyfernet.org**

Families and Work Institute is a non-profit organization that addresses the changing nature of work and family life. It is committed to finding research-based strategies that foster mutually supportive connections among workplaces, families and communities. **www.familiesandworkinst.org**

Forum for Youth Investment is a national initiative dedicated to increasing the quality and quantity of youth investments and youth involvement in the U.S. by promoting a big picture approach to planning and policy development. Its goal is to create strategic alliances among the full range of organizations that invest in youth. **www.forumforyouthinvestment.org**

The Innovation Center for Community and Youth Development's network of youth and adult staff and partners seek, test and promote innovative concepts and practices, providing tools for youth workers in diverse settings. **www.theinnovationcenter.org**

Foundations, Inc. operates extended-day enrichment programs and provides technical assistance to schools, school districts and other education and community organizations seeking to improve program performance and enhance student achievement in school and during non-school hours. **www.foundationsinc.org**

4-H Council works to build a world in which youth and adults learn, grow and work together as catalysts for positive change. 4-H serves youth through a variety of methods including organized clubs, school-enrichment groups, special interest groups, individual study programs, camps, school-age child care programs and instructional television programs. **www.fourhcouncil.edu**

The Future of Children is a journal published by the David and Lucile Packard Foundation. Its goal is to disseminate timely information on major issues related to children's well being, with special emphasis on providing objective analysis and evaluation, translating existing knowledge into effective programs and policies and promoting constructive institutional change. **www.futureofchildren.org**

Girls Inc. is a national non-profit youth organization dedicated to inspiring all girls to be strong, smart and bold. For over 55 years, Girls Inc. has provided vital educational programs to millions of American girls, particularly those in high-risk, underserved areas. **www.girlsinc.org**

HandsNet is dedicated to building the human services community on-line. Their new site provides daily headlines and action alerts from members, as well as information on the WebClipper service and expanded training capabilities. WebClipper automatically searches websites identified by experts in your field and ensures you never miss developments or resources vital to your work. **www.handsnet.org**

Middleweb offers a thorough online directory of programs and resources geared towards the improvement of after-school educational efforts. **www.middleweb.com/after-school.html**

National AfterSchool Association (NAA) (formerly the National School-Age Care Alliance, NAA) is a national membership organization supporting quality programs for school-age children and youth in their out-of-school hours. Established in 1987, NAA provides an umbrella organization to link people who work with school-age children and youth in a wide variety of agencies and settings. **www.naaweb.org**

National Association for the Education of Young Children (NAEYC) is the nation's largest organization of early childhood professionals and others dedicated to improving the quality of early childhood education programs for children birth through age 8. **www.naeyc.org**

National Association of Elementary School Principals' (NAESP) mission is to lead in the advocacy and support for elementary and middle level principals and other leaders in their commitment to all children. **www.naesp.org/index.jsp**

National Association of Child Care Professionals' (NACCP) mission is to provide leadership to those who build learning communities in response to individual and community needs. It does this by providing its members with national and regional training conferences and workshops; specialized periodicals, publications and products; opportunities for peer support and networking; and information and referral services. **www.naccp.org**

National Association of Resource and Referral Agencies (NACCRRA) is the national network of community-based child care resource and referral agencies. The organization is a common ground where families, child care providers and communities can share information about quality child care. **www.naccrra.org**

National Black Child Development Institute (NBCDI) advances a multi-faceted agenda to promote and protect the well being of all African-American children. NBCDI's wide range of programs respond to the necessity to replace the one-size-fits-all, deficit-oriented paradigm with initiatives that serve children based on their strengths and needs. **www.nbcdi.org**

National Child Care Information Center (NCCIC) was established to complement, enhance and promote child care linkages and to serve as a mechanism for supporting quality comprehensive services for children and families through dissemination and outreach. **www.nccic.org**

National Information Center for Children and Youth with Disabilities is the national information and referral center that provides information on disabilities and disability-related issues for families, educators and other professionals. Their special focus is children and youth (birth to age 22). **www.nichcy.org**

National Institute on Out-of-School Time (NIOST) is one of the nation's leading organizations focused on the importance of children's out-of-school time. Based at the Center for Research on Women at Wellesley College, NIOST has influenced policy, increased standards and professional recognition and spearheaded community action aimed at improving the availability, quality and viability of programs serving children and youth. **www.niost.org**

National Latino Children's Institute (NLCI) NLCI develops public education campaigns that create awareness of the needs and potential of Latino children. NLCI provides training and technical assistance on programs and policies that value young Latinos and help build healthy communities. **www.nlci.org**

National League of Cities (NLC) provides a wide range of programs and services to strengthen the ability of city officials to serve their communities. The Institute for Youth, Education and Families was launched in January 2000 as a special place within NLC to strengthen the capacity of municipal leaders to enhance the lives of children, youth and families. **www.nlc.org**

National Network for Child Care (NNCC)'s goal is to share knowledge about children and child care from the vast resources of the land grant universities with parents, professionals, practitioners and the general public. **www.nncc.org**

Section 7

National Resource Center for Health and Safety in Child Care includes information on state regulations for child care centers, plus extensive links on specific health and safety issues. **http://nrc.uchsc.edu**

The National Service-Learning Cooperative Clearinghouse is a searchable database offering information and resources to individuals and programs engaged in service-learning. **www.servicelearning.org**

National Youth Development Information Center (NYDIC) provides practice-related information about youth development to national and local youth-serving organizations at low or no cost. **www.nydic.org**

Open Society Institute & Soros Foundations Network offers a resource center of publications and articles concerning the advocacy of after-school programs. **www.soros.org/resources/articles_publications/publications/ideas_after-school_20020301**

The Out-of-School Time Learning and Development Project, an initiative of the Harvard Family Research Project, works to identify areas of challenge and opportunity in the emerging after-school field. Through this initiative, the Harvard Family Research Project builds on its expertise in evaluation and knowledge development to improve evaluation work and promote greater conversation and knowledge-sharing about evaluation among practitioners, policy-makers, funders, researchers and evaluators in the after-school field. **www.gse.harvard.edu/hfrp/projects/after-school/about.html**

SAC-L Listserv is an electronic discussion list that joins email users in a world-wide discussion of issues in school-age care (co-sponsored by NIOST and ERIC/EECE). **http://ericps.ed.uiuc.edu/eece/listserv/sac-l.html**

Search Institute is an independent, non-profit, non-sectarian organization advancing the well being of adolescents and children by generating knowledge and promoting its application through research and evaluation, publications, practical tools, training and technical assistance. **www.search-institute.org**

School-Age Notes is a resource organization that develops and provides information, technical assistance and resources concerning children and youth in out-of-school settings before and after-school and during vacations. **www.AfterSchoolCatalog.com**

Tufts University Child & Family Web Guide offers a directory of various after-school care and educational program resources. **www.cfw.tufts.edu/viewtopics.asp?categoryid=3&topicid=134**

The Tutor/Mentor Connection is a network of volunteers and organizations that works together to build the capacity, availability and quality of tutor/mentor programs in Chicago and around the country. **www.tutormentorconnection.org**

Quilt: Quality in Linking Together: Early Education Partnership is a national training and technical assistance project funded by the federal Head Start and Child Care Bureaus. Its purpose is to support full-day, full-year partnerships among child care, Head Start, pre-kindergarten and other early education programs at the local, state, tribal, territorial and regional levels. **www.quilt.org**

Public Awareness and Support

AfterSchool Alliance is an alliance of public, private and non-profit groups committed to raising awareness and expanding resources for after-school programs. **www.afterschoolalliance.org**

California Tomorrow has created the Access and Equity in After-School Programs Project to increase attention and dialogue about effective policies and practices in the after-school field related to improving educational and social outcomes for low-income and minority youth and communities. This project has a specific focus on the implementation of the 21st Century Learning Centers. **www.californiatomorrow.org/projects/cts.pl?project_id=2**

Center for Law and Social Policy (CLASP) is a national non-profit organization with expertise in both law and policy affecting the poor. Through education, policy research and advocacy, CLASP seeks to improve the economic security of low-income families with children and secure access for low-income persons to our civil justice system. **www.clasp.org**

The Children's Defense Fund works to educate the nation about the needs of children and encourage preventive investment in children. In addition to projects and publications, the Children's Defense Fund Update E-mail Network is available to child advocates, policymakers, community leaders, service providers, religious leaders and others interested in receiving regular updates and information on children's issues via email. **www.childrensdefense.org**

The Child Care Partnership Project website is designed to provide practical information on creating and maintaining public-private partnerships to increase and improve child care in states and communities throughout the country. It draws from the experiences of successful partnerships at the national, state and local levels to provide tools and materials for existing and future initiatives. **http://nccic.org/ccpartnerships/whatpppdo.htm#4**

Do Something is a nationwide network of young people who know they can make a difference in their communities and take action to change the world around them. As part of Do Something, young people are asked what they want to do to make things better and then are given the resources and support to bring their unique vision to life. **www.dosomething.org**

Fight Crime Invest in Kids is a national anti-crime and advocacy organization led by police chiefs, prosecutors and crime survivors that conducts and interprets research on how to keep children from becoming criminals. **www.fightcrime.org**

I Am Your Child is a national public awareness and engagement campaign to make early childhood development a top priority for our nation. **www.iamyourchild.org**

Keeping Kids on Track Campaign seeks to expand public awareness of the critical need for out-of-school time programs and to increase the public and private support for those programs. **www.kkot.org**

New England Workforce Partners is a joint endeavor by the six New England states to address the difficulty of attracting and retaining qualified staff to care for children. NEW Partners will create a model for regional data collection and analysis that can be used to better inform policy makers, providers, parents and researchers – ultimately improving the quality of care young children receive. **www.muskie.usm.maine.edu/newpartners**

Stand For Children is a national organization helping grassroots children's activists build Children's Action Teams which improve children's lives through successful policy change, awareness-raising and service initiatives. **www.stand.org**

USA Child Care unites child care providers in determining the future direction and accessibility of quality affordable child care for low and moderate-income families. It represents and works with active statewide organizations of providers across the country to ensure they are informed and engaged and is an active advocate providing expertise to legislators and policy makers about how to develop a system of high-quality child care. **www.usachildcare.org**

Professional Development

Bringing Yourself to Work: Caregiving in After-School Environments is a training model for after-school program staff that enables them to integrate self-knowledge and personal experience into their relationships with adults and children. **www.bringingyourselftowork.com**

The Center for Child Care Workforce is a non-profit, research, education and advocacy organization committed to improving child care quality by upgrading the compensation, working conditions and training of child care teachers and family child care providers. **ww.ccw.org**

National Association of Child Care Professionals seeks to improve, enhance and strengthen the credibility of the people who lead the child care industry by providing membership services and benefits. **www.naccp.org**

The National Association of Child Care Resource and Referral Agencies (NACCRRA) is a non-profit organization dedicated to providing the most up-to-date and useful information to parents seeking child care, child care professionals, NACCRRA members and child care advocates. **www.naccrra.net/default.htm**

National Association for Family Child Care (NAFCC) works to provide technical assistance to family child care associations by developing leadership and profession-alism, addressing issues of diversity and by promoting quality and professionalism through NAFCC's Family Child Care Accreditation. **www.nafcc.org**

Education Links

America Reads Challenge calls on all Americans to support teachers and help ensure that every American child can read well and independently by the end of third grade. America Reads offers training guides for tutors, tips for parents and information on reading initiatives across the country. **www.ed.gov/inits/americareads/index.html**

Appalachian Educational Laboratory (AEL) is a U.S. Department of Education lab serving Kentucky, Tennessee, Virginia and West Virginia. **www.ael.org**

The Educational Resources Information Center (ERIC) is a national information system designed to provide users with ready access to an extensive body of education-related literature. The ERIC database, the world's largest source of education information, contains nearly a million abstracts of documents and journal articles on education research and practice. **www.eric.ed.gov**

The Education Alliance at Brown University is a U.S. Department of Education lab serving Connecticut, Maine, Massachusetts, New Hampshire, New York, Rhode Island, Vermont, Puerto Rico and the Virgin Islands. The program focuses on measuring students' learning against standards and seeking to improve the effectiveness of schools. **www.lab.brown.edu**

Laboratory for Student Success (LSS) at Temple University is a U.S. Department of Education lab serving Delaware, Maryland, New Jersey, Pennsylvania and Washington, D.C. LSS is the lead laboratory in the specialty area of educational leadership. **www.temple.edu/lss/**

Mid-Continental Regional Educational Laboratory (McREL) is a U.S. Department of Education lab serving Colorado, Kansas, Missouri, Nebraska, North Dakota, South Dakota and Wyoming. McREL offers a searchable compendium of standards and benchmarks for K-12 education on their website. **www.mcrel.org**

National Center for Community Education promotes community education by providing leadership training to people who are interested in community schools, implementing community education or are 21st CCLC grant recipients. **www.nccenet.org**

National Council for Accreditation of Teacher Education (NCATE) is the teaching profession's mechanism to help establish high quality teacher preparation. Through the process of professional accreditation of schools, colleges and departments of education, NCATE works to make a difference in the quality of teaching and teacher preparation. **www.ncate.org**

National Middle School Association serves as a voice for professionals, parents and others interested in the education and developmental needs of young adolescents. **www.nmsa.org**

North Central Regional Educational Laboratory (NCREL) is a U.S. Department of Education lab serving Illinois, Indiana, Iowa, Michigan, Minnesota, Ohio and Wisconsin. NCREL specializes in the educational applications of technology. **www.ncrel.org**

Northwest Regional Educational Laboratory (NWREL) is a U.S. Department of Education lab serving Alaska, Idaho, Montana, Oregon and Washington. **www.nwrel.org**

Pacific Resources for Education and Learning (PREL) is a U.S. Department of Education lab serving American Samoa, Commonwealth of the Northern Mariana Islands, Federated States of Micronesia, Guam, Hawaii, Republic of the Marshall Islands and the Republic of Palau. **www.prel.org**

SouthEastern Regional Vision for Education (SERVE) is a U.S. Department of Education lab serving Alabama, Florida, Georgia, Mississippi, North Carolina and South Carolina. **www.serve.org**

Southwest Educational Development Laboratory (SEDL) is a U.S. Department of Education lab serving Arkansas, Louisiana, New Mexico, Oklahoma and Texas. **www.sedl.org**

WestEd is a U.S. Department of Education lab serving Arizona, California, Nevada and Utah. **www.wested.org**

Federal Resources

Administration for Children and Families (ACF) is responsible for federal programs which promote the economic and social well-being of families, children, individuals and communities. **www.acf.dhhs.gov**

After-School.gov is a clearinghouse of federal resources that support out-of-school time providers, programs and advocates. It provides information to help parents understand the issues that face kids and teens and on how to fund, start and operate an after-school program. **www.after-school.gov**

The Child Care Bureau makes grants to states and tribes to assist low income families with child care. The Bureau has initiated a variety of activities to improve the quality, availability and affordability of child care across the country including the National Child Care Information Center, **http://www.nccic.org**. The Child Care Bureau administers the Child Care and Development Block Grant (CCDBG) program and provides technical assistance to the nation on a variety of topics related to child care. **www.acf.dhhs.gov/programs/ccb**

Forum on Child and Family Statistics/ChildStats.gov offers easy access to federal and state statistics and reports on children and their families, including: population and family characteristics, economic security, health, behavior and social environment and education. **www.childstats.gov**

U.S. Census Bureau offers a searchable database of Census 2000 information. **www.census.gov**

U.S. Department of Housing and Urban Development (HUD) supports the "Ounce of Prevention Program" (OPP) which helps local organizations in and around Federal Empowerment Zones and Enterprise Communities (EZ/ECs) link their public safety, community planning and youth development efforts to similar ones in surrounding neighborhoods. **www.hud.gov**

U.S. Department of Education (DOE) works to ensure equal access to education and to promote educational excellence for all Americans. DOE administers the 21st Century Community Learning Centers Program. **www.ed.gov**

Appendix B: Reproducible Templates

NOTE: Permission to reproduce the following activity planning templates is granted to instuctors and agencies who have purchased this guide.

- Daily, Weekly Planning Charts
- Linking Activities to Learning and Quality Standards
- Activity Plan Template
- Documenting Activities
- Satisfaction Survey
- KWL Chart

Daily, Weekly, Monthly and Yearly Planning Chart

Components of an After-School Program: A Planning Guide and Checklist

Daily	Monday	Tuesday	Wednesday	Thursday	Friday
Recreation/Play					
Homework Support					
Fitness and Health					
Three or more times per week					
Arts					
Literacy					
Social Competence					
Math Problem Solving					
One or more times per week					
Science					
Technology					

	JAN	FEB	MAR	APR	MAY	JUN	JUL	AUG	SEP	OCT	NOV	DEC
Once a month												
Planning w/children and youth												
Community Service												
Three times per year (minimum)												
Family Event												

Linking to Quality Standards and Learning Benchmarks [66]

Activity Title							
Description							
Core Content Area (check all that apply)	Math	Literacy	Science	Arts	Fitness/ Nutrition	Social Competence	Other
Skills for the New Economy (check all that apply)	Numeracy	Communication		Problem solving	Technology		Work w/others
Quality Standards	NAA			SACERS		OTHER	

	Standard	Grade/Age	Description
Benchmark or Learning Standard			
Benchmark or Learning Standard			
Benchmark or Learning Standard			

[66] Template adapted from Hampshire Educational Collaborative. Activity Planning template developed by Susan O'Connor.

Links to Learning: *A Curriculum Planning Guide for After-School Programs*

Sample Activity Plan Template

Title
_____

Description
_____

Objectives
_____

Intended Outcomes
_____

Special Materials and Tools
_____

Space Requirements
_____

Age/Group Size
_____

The Activity
_____

Incorporating Technology

Extensions and Continuations

Conclusions/Reflections

Documentation

Documentation Chart

Staff Member:

Date:

Activity Title:

Number of participants:

Time spent:

The reason you chose the activity:

Which programmatic goal or objective did it relate to:

What did the children and youth actually do during the activity?

Evidence that the activity goal/objective(s) were met:

Evidence that additional, unexpected objectives were realized by doing this activity.

Did you make any unplanned adjustments, extensions to the activity?
If so, did they work well? Recommendations?

Sample Satisfaction Survey

Activity
_____

This is how I felt about the activity
_____

😊　　😐　　☹️

What I like best was:
_____

Next time, I think you should...
_____

KWL CHART

What you Know	What you Want to learn	What you Learned

NOTES

Links to Learning: *A Curriculum Planning Guide for After-School Programs*